Strategic Planning for the Chiropractic Practice

Eighteen Step-by-Step Exercises to Create
a Professional Strategic Plan for the
Practice of Your Dreams

Michael R. Wiles, BS, MEd, DC

Dean
Northwestern College of Chiropractic
Northwestern Health Sciences University
Bloomington, Minnesota

JONES AND BARTLETT PUBLISHERS
Sudbury, Massachusetts
BOSTON   TORONTO   LONDON   SINGAPORE

World Headquarters
Jones and Bartlett Publishers
40 Tall Pine Drive
Sudbury, MA 01776
978-443-5000
info@jbpub.com
www.jbpub.com

Jones and Bartlett Publishers
Canada
6339 Ormindale Way
Mississauga, Ontario L5V 1J2
CANADA

Jones and Bartlett Publishers
International
Barb House, Barb Mews
London W6 7PA
UK

Jones and Bartlett's books and products are available through most bookstores and online booksellers. To contact Jones and Bartlett Publishers directly, call 800-832-0034, fax 978-443-8000, or visit our website www.jbpub.com.

Substantial discounts on bulk quantities of Jones and Bartlett's publications are available to corporations, professional associations, and other qualified organizations. For details and specific discount information, contact the special sales department at Jones and Bartlett via the above contact information or send an email to specialsales@jbpub.com.

Copyright © 2008 by Jones and Bartlett Publishers, Inc.

All rights reserved. No part of the material protected by this copyright may be reproduced or utilized in any form, electronic or mechanical, including photocopying, recording, or by any information storage and retrieval system, without written permission from the copyright owner.

This publication is designed to provide accurate and authoritative information in regard to the Subject Matter covered. It is sold with th understanding that the publisher is not engaged in rendering legal, accounting, or other professional service. If legal advice or othe expert assistance is required, the service of a competent professional person should be sought.

Library of Congress Cataloging-in-Publication Data
Wiles, Michael.
Strategic planning for the chiropractic practice / Michael Wiles.
   p. ; cm.
ISBN-13: 978-0-7637-5085-5 (alk. paper)
ISBN-10: 0-7637-5085-9 (alk. paper)
  1. Chiropractic--Practice. 2. Strategic planning. I. Title.
  [DNLM: 1. Chiropractic—organization & administration. 2. Planning Techniques. 3. Practice Management—organization & administration. 4. Private Practice—organization & administration. WB 905 W676s 2008]
RZ232.2.W55 2008
615.5'34068—dc22
       2007010542
6048

Production Credits
Executive Editor: David Cella
Production Director: Amy Rose
Editorial Assistant: Lisa Gordon
Production Assistant: Amanda Clerkin
Marketing Manager: Jen Bengtson
Composition: Spoke & Wheel, Jason Miranda
Cover Design: Anne Spencer
Printing and Binding: Malloy, Inc.
Cover Printing: Malloy, Inc.

Printed in the United States of America
11 10 09 08 07   10 9 8 7 6 5 4 3 2 1

*This book is dedicated to my father,
Robert A. Wiles, 1926–1986,
who taught me the value of education,
industry, and proper preparation.*

Contents

Note to Readers ix
Preface xi

Chapter 1 What Is Strategic Planning? 1

Military Planning 3
Educational Planning 4
Industrial Planning 4
Survival of the Pioneers in the New Land 5

Chapter 2 Issues in Long-Range Planning 7

Long-Range Planning 7
    Internal Factors 8
    External Factors 8
    Time and Reality 9
    Adaptability Versus Stability: The Dynamic Plan 9
    Chief Cook and Bottle Washer (You…Yes, You) 10
    Controls and Statistics 11
Challenges in Planning 12

Chapter 3 Your Vision and Mission 13

Creating a Vision Statement 13
Creating a Mission Statement 16

Contents

Chapter 4	**Strategic Level Planning**	**25**

From Mission Statement to Strategic Goals 27

Chapter 5	**Tactical Level Planning**	**31**

Characteristics of Objectives 32
Creating Your First Objectives 34
Using Statistics 43
Managing Complex Strategic Plans 44

Chapter 6	**Operational Level Planning**	**49**

Translating Your Dream into Action 50
Creating Your Operational Plan 53
Organizing Your Plans 55

Chapter 7	**Doing First Things First**	**63**

Execution Plan A—Tactical Prioritization 64
Execution Plan B—Operational Prioritization 72

Chapter 8	**Daily Critical Action Steps**	**81**

Chapter 9	**Final Preparations**	**87**

Suggested Required Components of Your Strategic Plan 88
    New Patient Procedures 89
    Regular Visit Procedures 89
    Recall and Reactivation Procedures .91
    Promotion 95
    Fees 97
The Five Ps of Professional Success 99

Chapter 10	On Your Mark, Get Set 103
Appendix 1	Strategic Plan Example A 105
Appendix 2	Strategic Plan Example B 119
Appendix 3	Strategic Plan Template .135
Appendix 4	Executive Summary of Steps to Create Your Strategic Plan 145

One ship drives east and another drives west, with the self same winds that blow. 'Tis the set of the sails and not the gales which tells us the way to go.

—*Ella Wheeler Wilcox*

Note to Readers

This is a hands-on book about strategic planning. Read a chapter a day and complete the exercises, and in 10 days you will have created a detailed plan for developing the practice of your dreams. You don't see many books today that ask you to fill in written assignments, and I think that this is primarily because we live in a high-tech age of computers and personal digital assistants. I have noticed that today's chiropractic students rarely take written notes in class; they certainly do not take the copious and detailed notes that my generation was in the habit of creating. My feeling is that this tendency is wrong, and that *a magical attachment to concepts and ideas occurs in the transfer from hand to brain, in the art of writing.*

A Jewish tradition holds that it is a duty to write, by hand, a Torah scroll during one's lifetime. Certainly this was the way to pass on information in ancient times, and there is tremendous value in writing and seeing one's creative work in print. Recently, the art of journaling has become popular (again), and this may help us to rediscover the disappearing art of written correspondence and written memoirs.

For now, I ask for your indulgence. Whatever your inclination to skip the written exercises in this book, please persevere and complete them exactly as requested. Certainly, you may also type your work into your favorite computer program and create an entire plan in electronic format (which is actually advisable and, in fact, quite necessary to be able to amend the plan, print it, and distribute it). But initially, simply write out, in your own hand, the information I ask you to create.

Finally, I have used many quotes throughout the book, primarily as motivational support for you to complete your work with passion. Some of the quotes are from authors in pre-enlightened times and refer only to the male gender. Please read the idea and not the words, and do not look unkindly upon my work in this regard, as I have taken every effort to create a gender-neutral book.

> Reduce your plan to writing.... The moment you complete this, you will have definitely given concrete form to the intangible desire.
>
> —*Napoleon Hill*

Preface

Doctor, do you have a written mission statement that guides all activities of your practice? How about a clear vision of where your practice is headed in the future? Do you know specifically what you need to do tomorrow and the next day to achieve your purpose as a chiropractor?

Could you imagine a successful corporation that operated without a strategic vision or purpose? In the competitive, service-oriented world of the twenty-first century, operating a successful organization without a carefully designed strategic plan based on an established mission statement is probably impossible. You would be very unlikely to invest in a company that operated this way. Operating without a plan usually means wasting resources and energy on random activities—or what are often called "dead end activities"—with hopes of short-term gains.

My research indicates that only 5 to 10 percent of chiropractors actually have a written plan for success, and many of these are not useful strategic plans at all. Often, they are simply "motherhood" statements that have little or no relevance to the everyday activities of the practice.

Proper strategic planning begins with a clear vision of what you are aiming for, followed by the formulation of a mission statement—a written statement of what your practice stands for, what it values, and what it aims to achieve. While many of our practices have similarities regarding our values and aims, yours will no doubt have some unique characteristics that need to be expressed in your mission statement. I know that few chiropractors ever give this concept any thought at all, but those who do are well on their way to establishing a successful and purposeful practice.

Once your mission or purpose is established, you can develop your complete plan through the processes of strategic, tactical, and operational planning. This book has been designed to help you do this through a series of specific and ordered steps.

You will develop a mission statement and then use this statement to plan all of the steps necessary to move closer and closer to fulfilling your purpose in chiropractic. Your own individual mission and plan will be clearly articulated and developed. Your actions will become mission-oriented and not random acts of practice building and marketing. Done correctly, there should be nothing left to chance. For example, from time to time you probably have been visited by a salesperson with a particularly interesting product and promises of income if you are able to sell this product to your patients. Without a specific strategic plan, you often fall prey to this sort of offer. The next thing you know, you have a shelf full of product that is rapidly becoming dated. Eventually you discard the items or give them away for free or at discounted prices just to clear the shelf. Of course it seemed like a good idea at the time.

We've all done this, not only with products but also with services. I personally have been roped into long contracts for services and products that *seemed like a good idea at the time*. However, with a specific plan and course of action (which has been designed solely for the achievement of your mission), you will know *exactly* what products and services you need. In fact, you'll go out and contact the appropriate salespeople before they contact you! Done correctly, there should be nothing left to chance.

So—are you interested?

Read on, complete the exercises, and in a short time you'll have a specific plan of action, custom-built for you and your practice. This plan will guide you toward the attainment of the mission and goals you have set for yourself.

It's time—time to fulfill your own specific mission and purpose, time to define your practice mission and set it apart from others, time to develop a specific action plan to develop and grow your practice, *time to take control*.

> Nothing is more terrible than activity without insight.
>
> —*Thomas Carlyle (1795–1881)*

> Dig the well before you thirst.
>
> —*Asian proverb*

Chapter 1
What Is Strategic Planning?

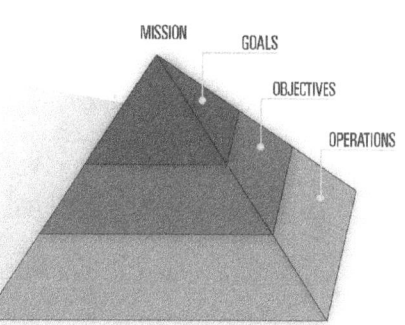

A plan is defined as "anything that involves selecting a course of action for the future."

Within the field of management, you can find a considerable body of knowledge pertaining to planning. You may have seen management textbooks and articles that emphasize a particular aspect of the planning process. All in all, it can be a very confusing topic for many reasons, among which is the use of terminology such as *goals, objectives, strategies, tactics, plans, policies,* and *procedures.*

In this book, we're going to develop plans based on a simple three-tiered model. The definitions we will use will make sense as you work through the development of your own plan, but here is a word of warning: don't get too hung up over the definition of a particular term. If, for example, you find that the use of the words *goal* and *objective* is the opposite of the way you have previously used them, by all means, interchange them. Just don't let your definitions block you from taking the action steps necessary to work your plan. Frankly, it does not matter what you call these steps as long as you develop a plan for yourself. However, having said that, I would like to emphasize that I will use these terms as they are commonly used in the art and science of strategic planning. It would certainly help you to adopt the current use of these terms.

There are at least five major reasons why it is absolutely necessary for you to develop a planning document for your practice.

1. Planning enables your practice to cope with change, and we have certainly all seen many significant changes in practice in recent years.
2. Planning creates adaptability for your practice, allowing you to ensure that your organizational objectives are reached or changed as necessary.

3. Success is sometimes defined as "moving toward a worthy goal or ideal." Notice the two components: a worthy goal and movement (or action). Strategic planning helps your practice to succeed because you will actually define your specific goals (or ideals) and the specific action steps to take to move you toward your goals.
4. Planning helps you with the day-to-day decision making in your practice.
5. Planning enables you to maintain an effective control process. Your statistics will now accurately reflect your progress toward your specific goals.

Our three-tiered model is based on traditional organizational planning and can be used in military, educational, industrial, and professional practice planning (**Figure 1-1**). As you will see, even nature uses this structure for planning.

At the top of our planning diagram is Mission. Actually, another step called Vision is above this, but we'll have more to say about vision statements later. For now, the top of your planning pyramid is your mission statement. This is the most important step, without which the rest of the structure is random at best and meaningless at worst. For this reason, it is also dangerous to use a packaged mission statement or to copy someone else's mission statement. Using a copied mission statement is probably better than having none, but you will end up achieving someone else's results, not your own (if you achieve anything at all—it's not easy to get passionate about someone else's mission).

Developing naturally out of your mission are your goals. Goals are broad areas of mission accomplishment and constitute the *strategic* level of planning. Ordinarily you will have only three to five goals, although the number can vary somewhat. Each goal will be subdivided into objectives. We will discuss objectives later in detail, but for now, it is important to know that each goal will be broken down into two to five objectives. This constitutes the *tactical* level

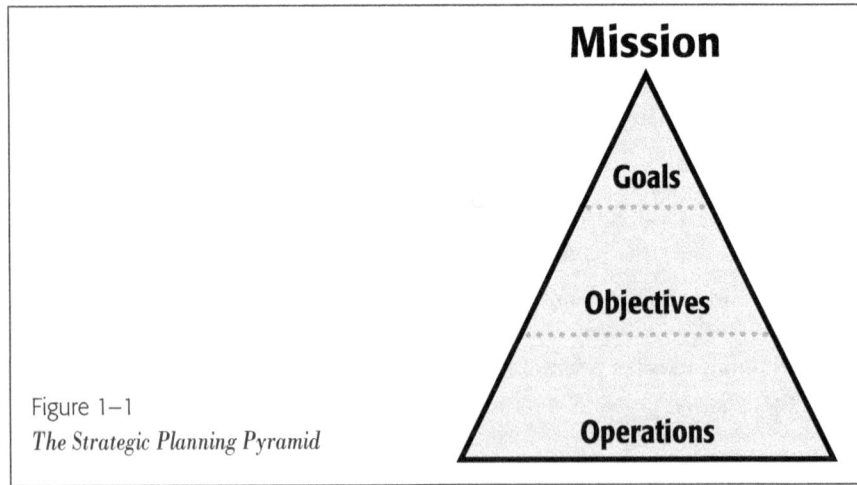

Figure 1-1
The Strategic Planning Pyramid

of planning. Finally, each objective (which is a specific and measurable target) is carefully analyzed and broken down into a number of necessary action steps. This constitutes the *operational* level of planning, and the steps are called operations, tasks, or plans. You could have any number of operations for each objective, but on average, you will have four to six.

My first strategic plan for my own practice many years ago had 1 mission, 4 goals, 14 objectives, and 81 operations. So you can see how this process creates a pyramid of planning levels, giving you a number of very specific tasks on which to concentrate.

To get a better concept of these planning levels and their utility, let me give you a number of examples in other fields.

Military Planning

Clearly, the specific interests and concerns of the various personnel are related to their planning level. Successful achievement of the mission can only occur when all members of the planning unit are working effectively on their portion of the overall picture.

As a specific example from World War II, a mission might be to "successfully liberate Europe." One goal of that mission would be to "stage a successful landing of forces in Normandy." An objective of that goal would be to "establish a beachhead at Omaha beach." That objective would be achieved by a number of plans, among which might be to "land a squad of troops at coordinates AB123 and disable the enemy bunker adjacent to the beach at that point." You can see that each successive level lower on the planning pyramid has a more specific task. Also, each level is only concerned with its specific target. Planning for your practice is no different, and you can see why specific targets are not achievable without proper planning. In your practice, for example, you may find the general (you) worrying too much about something the sergeant (your chiropractic assistant [CA]) should be concerned with.

Table 1–1 *Military Planning Levels*

Strategic Planning Level	Military Level	Officers
Goals (strategic)	Division	General staff
Objectives (tactical)	Regiment	Colonel, major
Operations (plans)	Squad, battalion	Sergeant, lieutenant

Table 1–2 *Education Planning Levels*

Strategic Planning Level	Educational Level	Officials
Goals (strategic)	Institutional	Dean
Objectives (tactical)	Departments, divisions	Department/division heads
Operations (plans)	Courses	Teachers, professors

Educational Planning

In the case of chiropractic education, a board and other executive officers oversee the mission. This mission is given as a strategic directive to the dean's level for planning. Tactical objectives are fulfilled by each of the various divisions and departments, and ultimately the individual professors are responsible for delivering the necessary information in their courses. Using this model, you can see how confusing the process would be if, for example, individual professors took it on themselves to deliver information that did not fit within the parameters of the overall strategic plan. Again, you can see parallels to your own practice.

Industrial Planning

The overall strategic direction of the company is determined by the board of directors and/or the owner of the company. This mission statement is then brought to life through the strategic goals of the company, overseen by the vice presidents. Various managers are responsible for particular tactical areas of production and marketing, and the plant supervisors marshal the efforts of the individual workers toward accomplishment of specific tasks.

The challenge for you is to begin thinking of your practice as a much larger operation than it may be at the present time. You are now the president and CEO of your practice, and your first step is going to be the clear enunciation of a meaningful mission statement, motivated by your vision of how you see

Table 1–3 *Industrial Planning Levels*

Strategic Planning Level	Company Level	Officials
Goals (strategic)	Upper management	Vice president
Objectives (tactical)	Middle management	Manager
Operations (plans)	Lower management	Foreman, supervisors

yourself contributing to the world. Once this is done, you will be planning all the necessary steps to ensure successful achievement of your goals. At the beginning, it may only be you wearing the hats of all the various officials and managers. Your goal may (or should) include growing your practice to the point where you can properly use your skills at the strategic level, with subordinates charged with the responsibility of fulfilling tactical and operational roles.

Survival of the Pioneers in the New Land

I added this unlikely example to show that even life-oriented activities can follow a strategic structure. Also, this particular example illustrates the time lines of the various portions of the strategic plan. In this case, survival is an ongoing process, and the strategic goals all relate to the process, or mission, of survival. They are long-term goals. In fact, strategic-level plans are typically in the 1- to 5-year time period. The original Soviet Union was known for its 5-year plans, which were simply strategic initiatives.

Tactical planning for the achievement of objectives usually has a time period of 60 to 120 days. Interestingly, in this example, the seasons are appropriate tactical-objective periods. Most organizations develop their strategic plans around the achievement of quarterly objectives, and this is an excellent basis for planning your own objectives.

Operational activities (tasks, plans, and operations) are usually daily or weekly activities. This example is a useful metaphor for helping you develop your own strategic plan.

Finally, within the scope of operational planning are the routine activities of running a practice. Among these are the activities that can be classified as policies, from which are derived procedures, from which are derived rules.

> To be in hell is to drift, to be in heaven is to steer.
>
> —George Bernard Shaw

Table 1–4 *Pioneer Planning Levels*

Strategic Planning Level	Company Level	Time Period
Goals (strategic)	Conquer new lands, build log cabin, clear land for farming	Lifetime
Objectives (tactical)	Prepare for winter, sow crops, harvest crops	Seasonal
Operations (plans)	Prepare meals, fetch water, chop firewood	Daily

Chapter 2

Issues in Long-Range Planning

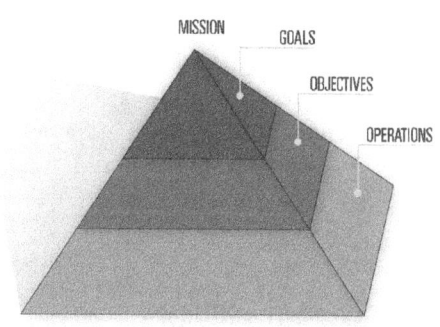

Long-Range Planning

You will deal with a number of challenges as you go through the exercises to develop your own plan. Being aware of these in advance will help alleviate the anxiety you may feel as you commit yourself to a plan on paper.

> Our plans miscarry because they have no aim. When a man does not know what harbour he is making for, no wind is the right wind.
>
> —Seneca
> (4 BCE–65 CE)

First, you will have to be very clear on your organization's basic mission. This includes knowing your clients, your competition, and your organization's place in the *big picture*. A part of this assessment is the determination of what constitutes your competitive advantage. Are you able to identify what you do best? For what are you known? You can find many ways to do this type of assessment; some management references suggest doing a *SWOT* analysis, for example.

SWOT is an acronym for strengths, weaknesses, opportunities, and threats. Obviously you want to recognize and capitalize on your strengths, identify your weaknesses as targets for improvement, look for and recognize opportunities for growth and development, and know what threats you face so you can be prepared for challenges that will always arise (usually when you least expect them).

A SWOT analysis can be an excellent starting place in the strategic planning process, especially if you feel somewhat disconnected from your practice and have begun to wonder what is wrong with it, or feel you are losing control. Honesty is critical as we pursue the planning process in earnest. This is your document, and total honesty is mandatory for it to be realistic, attainable, and a source of lasting passion for you.

You can begin by taking a totally honest look at factors both internal and external to the practice.

Internal Factors

You should begin to identify your strengths and weaknesses by looking within your practice at the areas in which you should (ideally) have considerable, if not total, control. Typical areas to analyze include your finances (assets, liabilities, and cash flow); physical plant and other material resources; your current office procedures and practice management procedures; your own skills, knowledge, and attitude, and those of your practice team members; the characteristics of your patient population; and your outcome measures, such as patient satisfaction, clinical results, and patient referrals.

Analyzing these factors can be a difficult process, especially if you have not confronted some of the weaknesses of the practice. Rest assured though, that identification of your weak areas is a valuable and necessary starting place as you begin the journey toward the fulfillment of your vision and mission. Getting input, where appropriate, from your practice team members, key advisors, and patients will give you a good idea of your current situation with respect to strengths and weaknesses.

External Factors

You identify opportunities and threats by looking at factors external to your practice. These factors include the political and legal environment, the social context of your practice, and the current state of the profession in terms of technological developments, professional trends, and market factors.

Other chiropractors can be competitors or noncompetitors. In some cases, they could be both. For example, one of your best friends and trusted colleagues might also be in practice across the street. This does not preclude his or her practice from being considered in your analysis of opportunities and threats. In addition to chiropractors, many other types of health providers and industries could be considered competitors for the same patient market, and these must be identified and understood as much as possible.

One of the simplest ways to initiate a SWOT analysis is to meet with your team members and simply ask them (and yourself) a few questions. What is special about our practice? Where are we running into problems? What makes us different from other practices? What are we worried about, now and in the future?

Time and Reality

It is very important to have a realistic time span for the strategic plan. By understanding the examples I have given, you can see that strategic planning is generally measured in years, tactical planning in months, and operational planning in days or weeks. This simple guideline is very valuable.

A realistic appraisal of your professional history is also important. In other words, it will be helpful if you have an honest and useful understanding of what has been important to your practice in the past and what will be important in the future. Of course, this also requires an honest appraisal of likely future circumstances. In other words, if you are currently 55 years old, it would not likely be a wise decision to have a long-term strategic goal for your practice with a 30-year time frame.

Although it may be time consuming, it is a very useful exercise (and one that is done by major organizations) to develop alternative future scenarios. In other words, based on your honest appraisal of your particular circumstances, you choose to follow Plan A. However, in the case of Event X or Event Y occurring, you are able to adapt quickly to Plan B. This kind of planning would have been extremely helpful for the practices that were most affected by the advent of Managed Care through the 1990s.

Adaptability Versus Stability: The Dynamic Plan

The planning process is a dynamic one, and plans are never *etched in stone* (even strategic plans). You are free to review and alter your overall plan as often as necessary to achieve your overall strategy. It is rumored that one very large international corporation reviews its mission statement every single week to ensure continued relevance. However, having said this, bear in mind that the higher an item is on the strategic planning pyramid, the more unlikely it is to change (or, rather, the more important it is to be stable and unchanging). Adaptability is one thing, but stability is another, and it is extremely important that the vision and mission statements are drafted carefully and after considerable thought so that they will give you a stable base for creating the rest of your plan.

You could imagine the confusion that would result if, during World War II, the leaders of the country changed their original mission, even after all of the organization and logistics were created to achieve it. Unfortunately, this is basically what happens to some chiropractic practices when, unwittingly, the doctor changes the overall strategic direction of the practice without fully comprehending the ramifications of such a change.

An example would be the sudden (and unplanned) introduction of a completely different technique system or practice management system. Many of us have been guilty of this error in judgment when we return from a particularly interesting postgraduate weekend seminar. Of course, changes such as these can certainly be introduced into any practice, and this is precisely where the process of strategic planning is necessary. Properly thought out, just like a military campaign, a strategic plan can be structured to create any future scenario you wish.

Chief Cook and Bottle Washer (You...Yes, You)

Tactical and operational planning occurs at the middle-management level or below. In the military, this means that the generals are happy to rely on the colonels to develop their own tactical plans, once they have been given the objective. In business, the vice president gives the managers the objective, and the managers work out the tactical details, leaving specific tasks to the line supervisors or foremen to develop. The responsibility level of the officers matches their strategic level in the organization.

Unfortunately, in practice, the doctor (or strategic-level planner) often creates the plans and methods of execution of all levels, bypassing other practice team members. In a small practice, the doctor is the general, the colonel, and the private, literally responsible to himself or herself for executing his or her plans. Further, mostly due to lack of appreciation of proper planning, the doctor will tend to plan in isolation, without the valuable input of other team members.

Then the doctor will wonder why the CA does not do the recall or reactivation calls as expected or does not use the appropriate script at all times. You can see how important it is to be able to create (and expect) responsibility at all levels of the planning pyramid.

Controls and Statistics

A critical step in the planning process is the determination of what controls will be necessary. The usual form of a control in the context of strategic planning for chiropractic practices is a statistic. Typically, doctors keep statistics of various aspects of their practices for odd reasons. Either they have been told that a particular statistic actually measures their progress in a specific area, or more likely they are taking a periodic measurement to compare themselves with others or the national average. After you have completed your own strategic plan, you will see that the necessary controls (statistics) are totally obvious and forthcoming directly from your plan.

In the military example in Chapter 1, if you were the general in charge of the mission, what statistics would you demand of your officers and enlisted personnel? It would depend on whether the statistics were derived from a tactical or operational level, for one thing. You would not expect a sergeant to tell you how the entire regiment was performing. Of course, the strategic level yields only qualitative results—either the landing succeeded or it did not succeed. As you get lower in the planning process, statistics become more obvious and more specific. As a general rule, your main statistics will be derived from the tactical level, since one of the characteristics of an *objective* is, in fact, that it is *objective*, or measurable (otherwise we would call them *subjectives* rather than objectives).

A properly run organization is a cybernetic system, which means that it operates by feedback in a continuous loop. Using systems theory, it then follows that any measure of the operation of the system gives you an idea of the whole system's performance. It's like saying that on a given expressway, the traffic can only go as fast as the slowest car. In a closed system operating this way, all you would have to do is measure any car's speed and it would show you how the whole expressway was performing. In this way, if you carefully choose your controls, or statistics, you will be able to get an accurate perspective of your overall practice performance.

Challenges in Planning

> Wishing consumes as much energy as planning.
> —Anonymous

You must concentrate on the present even though you are planning for the long-term. In other words, there must be a clear link between now and then. It is a mistake to create a future scenario that has no relevance at all to current activities. If really dramatic change is planned, you need to create either an intermediate plan or a de novo organization. Think in terms of a physical time line: You are *here* now, and you want to go *there* then. Planning must be on a continuum from the present to the future with an actual line between these two points.

Do not confuse a "planning study" with a plan. You are not just creating a hypothetical future as part of a "wish" campaign. You must be prepared to commit time and resources for a plan to work.

One of the biggest challenges in strategic planning is the creation of clear, attainable, and specific objectives. We will talk more of this later as you complete the planning exercises.

> We must ask where we are, and whither we are tending.
> —Abraham Lincoln

Avoid placing too much emphasis on economic or technological factors. Of course they need to be considered, but both of these factors can change rather quickly, and a plan that is too dependent on them may become obsolete. An example would be building a large part of your practice around existing technology in a specific area, such as subluxation detection technology or radiographic technology. In these cases, you have little control over the technology that may or may not keep up with trends in the industry. Also, be realistic with economic factors but avoid overemphasis on such changeable items as professional fees or your own cash flow.

Chapter 3

Your Vision and Mission

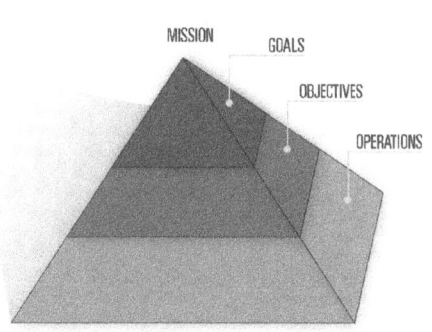

At the top of the planning pyramid is your mission. During the 1990s, the term *mission statement* lost some popularity and in many management books was replaced by the term *purpose statement*. Remember what I said earlier: Do not get hung up on the semantics. It does not matter what you call it, as long as you recognize that a broad philosophic statement oversees the planning process, based solely on what is in your heart and your head. You can call this your mission, your calling, your purpose, or even your passion statement if you want.

In 1987, Peter Block introduced the concept of another corporate document called the *vision statement*. He said that while the mission statement describes what business we are in, a vision statement "is an expression of hope," a vision "of how we would like the organization to be."

In our planning model, you will develop both a vision statement and a mission statement. Think of the planning pyramid and envision at the pinnacle of the pyramid a mission statement. Overhead is a star, which is your guiding light, your vision statement.

> Quo vadis
> (whither goest thou)?
>
> —*Dr. Joseph Janse,
> at a National College
> of Chiropractic
> graduation ceremony*

Creating a Vision Statement

Your vision statement is a very short summary of the values, expectations, and passion you bring to your practice. It is necessary to crystallize and communicate your values and expectations in a vision that others can easily grasp, so that they will be able to manage the leap from mission statement to

Chapter 3 Your Vision and Mission

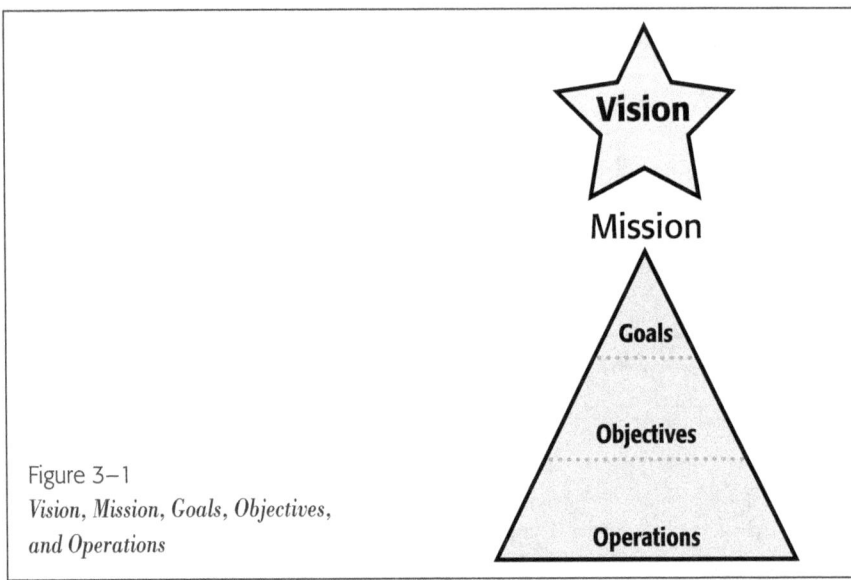

Figure 3–1
Vision, Mission, Goals, Objectives, and Operations

mission-driven action. Even if you are working alone or with only one assistant, you will be able to refer to your vision as a rock on which to anchor and stabilize your practice during periods of uncertainty.

Read the following examples of vision statements:

- Universal access to high-quality chiropractic care
- Everyone deserves and needs chiropractic care
- Wellness without barriers
- Enhancing the lives of as many people as possible
- Optimal health equals optimal spine
- I am a chiropractic master
- Chiropractic fully integrated in the health-care system
- We have the most unique practice in the world
- A subluxation-free world, one patient at a time

Vision has many definitions, some of which include the ability to anticipate and make provisions for future events, insight, imagination, a vividly imagined thing or state, and something very beautiful or pleasing (*Funk and Wagnalls Dictionary*).

Your first exercise is simply to take whatever time it takes to envision exactly what it is that you see for yourself as a chiropractor. Use your insight and your imagination—vividly imagine your future as a beautiful and pleasing thing. Then describe in your own words what you see in your mind.

EXERCISE 1

Describe in one paragraph the essence of what it is you see as a visual representation of your passion for chiropractic.

Now that you have committed yourself to paper, you can reduce this paragraph to its most basic meaning. It is very important that you do not become paralyzed by this exercise. By the time you have finished this planning process, you may indeed find that your original vision becomes more easily definable or that it changes or evolves into something else. This is not only to be anticipated but also to be welcomed. It is like learning to paint. You follow the step-by-step instructions, but as you become more skilled you create de novo works of art based on your own inner creativity. Expect this to happen. For now, work through the exercises with a vision that you can start with and, if it changes, then welcome the insight and go back to exercise 1 again. If it does not change, then you know you have discovered a lasting vision on which you can depend.

EXERCISE 2

Reduce your vision statement to one sentence that incorporates its general essence. Your sentence should convey a powerful and meaningful statement to another person. Test it on a trusted friend or family member.

Chapter 3 Your Vision and Mission

> A task without a vision is drudgery. A vision without a task is a dream. A task with a vision is a victory.
> —Anonymous

When you are happy with the sentence you have created, I want you to try something. Do your best to reduce it even further to a phrase, a slogan, a credo, a motto, or a set of words (very few) that convey the essence of your vision. Two examples are the mottoes of Canada ("From sea to sea") and the United States ("In God we trust"). These convey a much larger concept or vision in very few words. From these visions one can develop a much larger agenda of goals and objectives, and the vision phrase becomes an icon for both reference and reverence.

EXERCISE 3
Write your vision in 10 words or less.

Developing a vision statement is not an easy thing to do. But by now you realize that the construction of a strategic plan places you miles above the ordinary practitioner who simply gets swept along by outside forces. Thomas Peters observed, "Developing a vision and values is a messy, artistic process." Remember that you are the CEO of your organization. So, where are you going? What are your values? How will you get there? Your plan will answer all these questions, starting with your vision.

> Every man without passions has within him no principle of action, nor motive to act.
> —Claude Adrien Helvetius
> (1715–1771)

Take the time to develop a vision statement that crystallizes your passion in chiropractic. Once this is done, you can begin working your way down through our strategic planning pyramid. (But remember: Nothing is ever etched in stone, so you always have the opportunity to change anything in your strategic plan.)

Creating a Mission Statement

Our next step is to develop a mission statement (or a purpose statement). This statement is not the same as step 1 in the development of your vision statement.

> *Exercise 1*
> My vision is to see people all over the world getting chiropractic care without political, legislative, or financial barriers. I see chiropractic practiced proudly and with the highest quality in every country and taught throughout the world. The best chiropractic care should not just be available to those who can afford it. I see chiropractic as an international force in health care!
>
> *Exercise 2*
> My vision is that chiropractic is practiced worldwide and that nobody should be denied the opportunity to get the best care possible!
>
> *Exercise 3*
> "Universal access to high-quality chiropractic care"

Figure 3–2 *An Example of the Development of a Vision Statement*

It is not simply an enlargement of your vision statement. It includes everything that is embodied in the vision statement, but it also includes the basis for your goals—the ultimate targets of your action plan. In other words, it brings the vision (of the future) into the mission (of the present).

Present (operational plans) ⟶ **Mission** ⟶ Future (vision)

In the earlier example of a World War II mission, the mission was "successfully liberate Europe," which implied action steps in the present. The vision might have been "freedom for all peoples of the world," which is a passionate reason for going forward but does not actually imply any particular action in the present. Make sure you understand this point and then proceed with the instructions for exercise 4.

The simplest definition of a mission statement is the purpose or reason for the organization's existence. It might be helpful to think of this as similar to the creation of a vision statement, in reverse. Starting with the vision statement, you will enlarge on it until it incorporates the type of practice you are building and the values you support. In other words, you will be describing the business and professional activities of the practice, as well as the human values that accompany them. In this way, you give all practice team members something to which they can be loyal.

These expressions of intent will serve as the foundation for your practice goals, objectives, operational plans, policies, procedures, and rules, as well as a basis for decision making and your expectations for individual behavior.

Chapter 3 Your Vision and Mission

It is sometimes helpful to break down the various components and stakeholders in the mission statement. Thinking of the mission statement as a basis for future action, you have four dimensions to consider:

- Economic factors
- Technological factors
- Political factors
- Social factors

> If one advances confidently in the direction of his dreams, and endeavors to live the life that he has imagined, he will meet with a success unimagined in the common hours.
>
> —Henry David Thoreau

Economic factors include specific market forecasting, consumer spending patterns, and the business investment climate. State-of-the-art technological forecasting is necessary to create adaptability to the constant changes in the technical arena. Political forces and factors are always important considerations in chiropractic planning, for example, the likelihood of legislative changes and how this will affect the delivery of care. Finally, social factors include a study of the changing values of society, the trends in lifestyle as well as demographic changes in your service radius.

Not all of these factors will necessarily be included in a mission statement. However, keep in mind as we go down the planning pyramid that the scope of each successive level gets narrower. You cannot suddenly incorporate something at the tactical level that is not included at the strategic level or above. So, your mission statement has to be carefully worded to include as much as possible about your practice in the fewest number of words. Think of Winston Churchill saying, "Never in the course of chiropractic history has so much been said by so few words."

Let's begin by listing the key ingredients of your mission statement.

EXERCISE 4

List the key words or phrases that are necessary to fully describe the way that your practice will seek to fulfill its vision.

(In the example in **Figure 3–2***, the key words or phrases might be* high-quality care, care for as many people as possible, international, barrier-free.*)*

Once you have developed this list, you will need to create one or more sentences that describe in simple language what the actual purpose of the practice is. You should begin by using the words "my mission or purpose is..."

EXERCISE 5
State your practice mission in one or more sentences.

My mission or purpose is...

What you have just written is the most important paragraph you may ever write in connection with your practice. Review it to make sure that it either contains everything you can ever envision doing in your practice or at least that it does not exclude anything you envision doing.

Many years ago, I remember hearing Dr. Karl Parker say that the three steps for developing a successful practice were desire, decision, and direction (spoken I might add with that wonderful Texas accent the Parkers are known for). These three steps correspond to your strategic pyramid levels of strategic planning (desire), tactical planning (decision), and operational planning (direction). All this has to emanate from the mission statement, so make sure that your final statement conveys the message of what you want and how you will get there.

There is no such thing as a bad mission statement. Clearly, some will be articulated in such a powerful way that you will want to read it or say it over and over again as a source of inspiration. However, whatever you come up with is better than nothing. More importantly, it is *your* own statement, constructed from *your* own vision. This is a very powerful beginning to your planning process.

Here are some examples of mission statements from chiropractic practices and chiropractic students I have had the privilege of teaching over the years. Naturally, you may use the ideas in them for working or reworking your own, but please make sure that your statement is from *your* heart only.

Example 1
Our mission and purpose is to adjust and educate as many people as possible toward optimum health through chiropractic care.

Example 2
Our mission and purpose is to provide a complete program of care to as many people as possible. Complete care includes the highest quality of chiropractic care as well as comprehensive health maintenance care.

Example 3
Our mission and purpose is to provide effective chiropractic care to as many families as possible.

Example 4
Our mission and purpose is to create and operate a holistic health care clinic in order to relieve pain in as many people as possible.

Example 5
Our mission and purpose is to build a fully organized holistic practice in order to diagnose, treat, and educate as many people as possible.

Example 6
Our mission and purpose is to create and build a chiropractic practice that improves and promotes health throughout my community.

Example 7
Our mission and purpose is to have a well-known and successful clinic in _____ (location), which is highly respected in both the public and health care community. Our clinic promotes health maintenance care and emphasizes individual responsibility in health and prevention.

Example 8
Our mission and purpose is to provide a family and wellness-oriented health service to people of all ages. Our clinic is part of an integrated health care team that emphasizes individualized care. We aim to contribute to the public awareness of chiropractic in preventing illness and maintaining optimal health.

Example 9
Our mission and purpose is to manage a highly successful subluxation-based practice with a focus on family care and with a specialty interest in sports injuries.

Example 10
Our mission and purpose is to develop and manage a chiropractic clinic with a worldwide reputation for excellence, and to be a first-class community resource center for natural health care.

Example 11
Our mission and purpose is to detect and correct spinal subluxations in as many families as possible.

Example 12
Our mission and purpose is to help as many families as possible to achieve optimal health through chiropractic care, in my community.

Example 13
Our mission and purpose is to operate three unique chiropractic clinics that have a worldwide reputation for excellence. The quality, effectiveness, and distinctiveness of our service are characterized by the delivery of highly skilled chiropractic adjustments within a truly caring atmosphere, as well as education and research about chiropractic and the healing process. Our aim is to enhance the lives of as many people as possible, through chiropractic and complementary natural healing methods.

Each of these examples reflects the personal strategic goals of its authors. I have provided these examples simply to give you an idea of the type of wording that your own mission statement may have. You can see that some of these statements have only one sentence; others use up to three sentences. Whenever possible you should aim for economy of words in the mission statement. However, do not feel constrained to do this. If necessary, simply write down everything that is in your heart about your mission and then try to reduce it to its essence.

Finally, to give you an idea of a corporate mission statement, I have included two mission statements of the Canadian Memorial Chiropractic College in Toronto, Canada. The first is a former mission statement, which was revised in recent years to the second statement. This is to show that an organization can reword its mission statement to reflect growth and change and to keep the terminology current without changing the essence of the statement.

Certainly you may find your own statement changing several times over the short term as you become conversant with the planning process and analyze your practice as you have never done before. If a large organization like a chiropractic college can do this, you can too.

> The mission of CMCC is to benefit society through the pursuit of knowledge and the education of chiropractors so that they may acquire the skills necessary to apply this knowledge and contribute effectively to the health care team. The goal of the educational program is to

graduate primary contact health care practitioners who are knowledgeable in the art, science, and philosophy of chiropractic; competent in clinical skills; and committed to educating and caring for their patients and their community and who reflect the common attitudes, values, and ethics of health care professions emphasizing the cooperative nature of the chiropractor–patient relationship.

—*Mission Statement from 1994–1995 academic prospectus*

It is the mission of the Canadian Memorial Chiropractic College to advance the art, science, and philosophy of chiropractic, to educate chiropractors, to further the development of the chiropractic profession, and to improve the health of society.

—*Mission Statement from 2003–2004 academic prospectus*

Clearly these are complex mission statements, but you can see how they contain all the necessary elements of human values and procedural and technological goals and how they would appeal to the community (patients), the clients (students), and the members (faculty). These very comprehensive statements also illustrate a number of ideas I suggest you include in a chiropractic practice mission statement:

- Primary function (in this case as an educational institution)
- Goals (again, in this case as related to an educational program)
- Relationship to community, profession, and society

Nonetheless, all of this is accomplished with only two sentences in the original statement and only one sentence in the revised statement!

One of my favorite institutional mission statements is that of Northwestern Health Science University, of which Northwestern College of Chiropractic is one of four educational programs. It, too, conveys a wealth of information about the values and purpose of the University, all within one sentence:

> The mission of Northwestern Health Sciences University is to advance and promote natural approaches to health through education, research, clinical services and community involvement.

At this point you have developed your own vision statement and mission statement. For many of you, this is the first time you have analyzed your strategic goal in this much detail. Congratulations! You are well on your way to creating a master plan for your successful practice. The next step is a critical one.

Imagine for a moment that you are Franklin Roosevelt in the Second World War. You have, along with your cabinet, decided on a vision, which is "freedom for all peoples of the world." Like all vision statements, this is a phrase that can mobilize emotion and passion but it says little about the current state of affairs. Therefore, you have created a mission statement that is rather long but contains the phrase, "successfully liberate Europe from tyranny, rebuild the infrastructure and economy, and reestablish democratic rule."

The next step is your plan to make this mission a reality. How would you do this?

Well, you would most likely break this mission down into specific goals, such as "land in Europe," "liberate France," "liberate the Low Countries," and so on. Then you would assign specific goals to specific individuals such as General Eisenhower, among others. You would then expect those individuals charged with a strategic goal to come back with a specific plan that included breaking their goal down into smaller objectives.

Your next job then as head of your practice is to take your mission statement and break it down into its inherent component parts, each of which will become a strategic goal.

Chapter 4

Strategic Level Planning

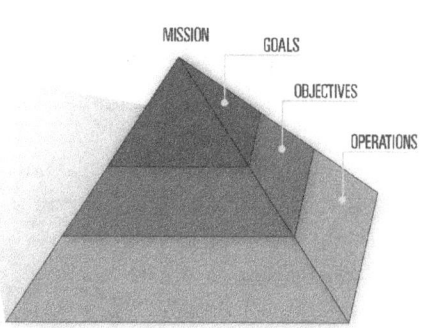

Goals are defined as "desired states of affairs that the organization attempts to realize."

They are levels of aspiration that are long-term and often timeless. Generally it is important that all members of the organization are in agreement with the strategic goals. Moreover, the goals of an organization should not change frequently. Certainly, as I have emphasized, nothing in the planning process is etched in stone. But keep in mind that the higher you are on the planning pyramid, the more that stability is important. In the world of business, strategic goals usually involve survival, efficiency, employee satisfaction, and the production of goods.

Note that in many management textbooks the terms *goals* and *objectives* are sometimes used interchangeably. In the context of the model presented here, the terms are quite independent of each other and have a very specific meaning. Please refer to **Figure 1-1** and the discussion that follows it for further clarification if you do not fully understand this point.

Before proceeding, I want to give a quick review of the process from this point onward.

In this chapter, as you develop your practice goals, you will work on a strategic level of planning with future desired states in mind. In the next chapter, you will learn about the tactical level of planning. You will take each of your goals and dissect them into specific objectives that have more relevance to the control of current operations in your practice. Finally, Chapter 6 covers the operational level, and you will take each of your objectives and dissect them into very specific tasks or operations.

Remember the statistics from my original plan: 1 mission, 4 goals, 14 objectives, and 81 tasks. This is only a guideline. You may end up with fewer or more than each of these, but as a rule, you should follow a similar pattern for realistic planning.

The further down the strategic planning pyramid you go, the more specific the scope and the more current the time frame. Using this model, you can see that a mission statement is very much concerned with the future, as is the vision statement (distant future).

So, are you ready to proceed? First, to review, fill in the blanks below:

My vision is:

My mission is:

One of the reasons I had you rewrite these statements is that by now you should have memorized them. They should flow naturally from your mouth every time you think about your practice. You need to write and rewrite them often until they are part of your inner being. Everything you do from now on in your practice is done with reference to these statements. If someone says, "Oh, you're a chiropractor, what do you do?" you can tell them what your purpose is and say it with passion and excitement. No longer will you use canned definitions or fumble for words.

"Why did you become a chiropractor?" Well, I'm glad you asked. My vision is...

You now have stability, starting in your own mind, describing who you are and why you are here. You will wake up each morning with the mission and purpose in mind, guiding you and motivating you each day to manage your practice like the magnificent organization it is, ever seeking to carry out the necessary tasks efficiently, and fulfilling your objectives so that your goals are achieved. It all makes so much sense.

From Mission Statement to Strategic Goals

I want you to take a close and neutral look at your mission statement and list the main items it includes. Think strategically now, like you are plotting a military campaign. You want nothing left to chance. Sometimes it helps to have someone assist you who is not connected with your practice or chiropractic at all. In this way, you may avoid the biases, prejudices, and limitations you bring to the table from your previous practice experience.

Some mission statements naturally flow into strategic goal areas. For example, CMCC's current mission statement actually lists its four goals in only one sentence. Northwestern's mission statement lists two primary goals ("advance" and "promote") within its one rich sentence. These are ideal mission statements. If your statement does not readily yield several goals, you may wish to go back a few steps and recheck your work up to this point. Generally speaking, one or more goals should practically jump out of a mission statement.

Let me give you an example.

Mission: To provide effective chiropractic care to as many people as possible.

If you were to ask a nonpatient and nonchiropractor their opinion as to how this mission could be accomplished, you would find that they might logically break it down into several goal areas. This is exactly what I did with this example, and here are the results:

1. You need to provide "effective chiropractic care," which means you need to have an office and staff, programs of care, and methods of knowing when the care is effective or not.
2. You need to educate your patients and the public so that they know when to come to see you. This is necessary if you intend to serve "as many people as possible."
3. To serve as many people as possible requires a community consciousness, so you should seek to identify and serve the health needs of the community.

4. To survive, you must be financially responsible not only for yourself and your family, but also for your staff and suppliers.

These are the four goal areas that were identified from the mission given above. After elaboration and brainstorming, these goal areas were reduced to the following four strategic goals:

1. To successfully treat our patients and restore their health to optimal levels
2. To educate our patients and the public about chiropractic
3. To serve the health needs of the community
4. To provide sufficient resources for the survival and growth of the practice and staff

Note that, as in the business world, these goals include the broad areas of survival, efficiency, employee satisfaction, and production.

Your job now is to complete this process with your own mission statement.

Brainstorming with others is an excellent method for completing this exercise. For those unfamiliar with the brainstorming technique, here is how it works. In a given time period, say 30 minutes, list every possible response to the problem, without regard for what may or may not be either possible or necessary. Aim for as large a list as possible, and simply keep writing as soon as an idea pops into your head. Do not judge any specific item or response as being good or better or inappropriate or silly—just write them all down.

Then, review the list and begin to discard items that are inappropriate, and regroup other items when possible. In true brainstorming, it is at this point that the members of the group would argue for or against inclusion in the final list. Presumably, the authors of any specific item would argue for inclusion and have to defend their items. Continue this elimination process until you reduce the list to the fewest and most important items.

EXERCISE 6

Analyze your mission statement and extract the major areas for goal development. As a general guideline, try to limit this list to between three and five goal areas. Do not try to word these as goals yet because this may limit your creativity. Simply list and describe the necessary components of your mission statement.

From Mission Statement to Strategic Goals

Chapter 4 Strategic Level Planning

How did you do?

Make sure you do not proceed until you are happy with the items you have listed above. When this is done, you need to reword the items into goal statements. Generally, a goal statement begins with the word *to* and represents a strategic initiative rather than a specific task. In the example on page 28, you will note that the items refer to general future needs of a practice that aimed to fulfill the indicated mission. Goals contain no references to specific requirements of office space, staffing, number of patients, and so on. This information comes later. For now, simply reword your goal areas into strategic goal statements.

EXERCISE 7
State your strategic goals.

The goals of my practice are:

1.

2.

3.

4.

5.

Chapter 5

Tactical Level Planning

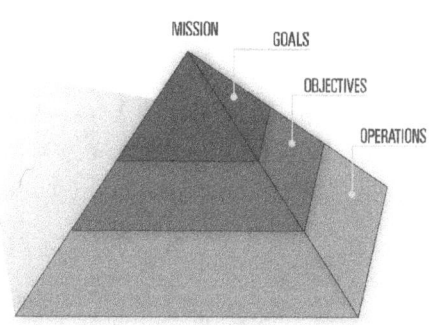

Congratulations. You've made great progress, and you are now at a critical step in the planning process. You are about to hand over your general's grand strategic goals to your regimental colonels for implementation as tactical objectives.

> To fail to exploit your achievements is ominous.
> —Lao Tzu

In the jargon of management experts, tactical planning "involves deciding specifically how the resources of the organization will be used to help the organization achieve its strategic goals."

The strategic level of planning (goals) deals primarily with uncertainty (of the future), and the operational level (plans and tasks) deals primarily with certainty (of the present). The tactical level (objectives) bridges the gap between the grand strategic goals and the actual day-to-day work of the practice. Some organizational textbooks refer to this middle ground as "coordinative planning."

This makes tactical planning very special, and a great deal of attention must be paid to the following exercises. This is where we begin to rein in our attention from the future and begin to set in motion the specific objectives that will force us to "put the rubber to the road." Up to this point, we have been dreamers; with tactical planning, we become planners and tacticians.

Chapter 5 Tactical Level Planning

Characteristics of Objectives

Tactical plans, or objectives, have several characteristics that make them unique in the planning process. Most management consultants agree on the following seven characteristics of objectives:

- Objectives must be specific and well understood by all members of the organization.
- Objectives must be balanced. That is, one objective should not be in competition with another objective. An example would be the natural conflict of quality control versus profits (or, quality versus quantity). The one wants to spend the resources of the organization and the other wants to save the resources. It is very important that your objectives are integrative and take into account the needs of all areas of your practice. How is this done? By constantly referring to the strategic goals. If there is still confusion as to the resolution of tactical conflict, refer the problem up the pyramid to the mission statement and, if necessary, up to the vision statement. You can see how important the process of strategic planning is in this example. Imagine some of the decisions you have made in the past that have been either misguided or miscalculated, because you had no planning reference point.
- The expected results must be clearly identified. You must be quite specific here. For example, your goal might be "to successfully treat our patients and restore their health to optimal levels" (considerable uncertainty, future focus, grand strategic goal). On the tactical level, you will have to specify exactly what this means. In other words, how do you define "successfully treat"? When will you know that you have accomplished this? What exactly does "optimal levels" mean? Also, the statistics that measure your practice are derived mostly from tactical objectives. Part of this exercise is to determine the exact, desired outcome of each strategic goal and tactical objective. This then becomes your necessary statistic. In the above example, the desired outcome could be defined as "patients who are scheduled and treated effectively." In other words, to successfully treat our patients, we would first have to book appointments, get them in the office, treat them, get them back for assessment, and so on. Accordingly, a statistic to measure this area might be "number of maintenance patients seen per month" (measures your effectiveness at maintaining optimal health levels) or "percentage of patients keeping their original appointments" (measures effectiveness of the booking and scheduling process). As you will see, this process seems to flow quite naturally once you have established your tactical objectives for each goal.

- Both internal and external constraints must be considered and accounted for. This means making sure that what you are planning is legal, ethical, and ultimately possible. Ideally, you should have considered potential legal, environmental, technical, fiscal, personnel, and ethical constraints when you created your mission statement (see page 19) and again as you formulated your strategic goals. However, regardless of this previous consideration, you should ensure that your objectives account for any serious potential constraints.
- Objectives must be measurable and quantitative, although some objectives by their nature do not lend themselves to quantitative measurement and by necessity will be qualitative. This is perhaps the most important characteristic of tactical objectives. Your mission and goals are qualitative (though some quantitative component is not necessarily forbidden), but it is at this intermediate level that the process becomes generally quantitative. Keep this in mind as you develop your objectives, because a natural consequence of this process is the evolution of the statistics you will be keeping.
- The objectives must be both realistic and feasible, especially for the members of the organization who will be carrying out the work. Management experts call this "within the power of the involved work unit." This implies that the objectives should pose neither too little a challenge nor too difficult a challenge. The former leads to apathy and lack of desire, and the latter leads to frustration and, more than likely, procrastination.
- Finally, the objectives must be acceptable to all members of the organization. A school of thought in management called "management by objectives" emphasizes the tactical level as being the most critical in organizational success and maintains that the greatest challenge in management is the balancing of the needs of individuals with the needs of the organization. An example of this in chiropractic practice occurs when the doctor suddenly decides that recall and reactivation are urgently required due to a slump in patient visits (sound familiar?). The doctor then mistakenly assumes that the CAs enjoy phoning inactive patients (and getting rejected over and over again). Sure, you can give them scripts and role-play, but the fact is, few doctors have taken the time to derive *all* of their practice procedures from their strategic plan (as you are doing), thereby ensuring that your objectives are acceptable to your staff right from the beginning.

Finally, consider the following checklist before you construct your objectives, and learn the five primary objectives of any organization:
- Identification (of the organization and its objectives)
- Integration (to meet the needs of individuals and the organization)

Chapter 5 Tactical Level Planning

- Collaboration (through a mechanism for the productive use of conflict and its control)
- Adaptation (to allow the organization to respond quickly and appropriately to change)
- Revitalization (for a continual planning process that enables you to deal with the constant issues of decay and growth)

> Management by objectives works if you know the objectives. Ninety percent of the time, you don't.
> — Peter Drucker

After creating your practice objectives you should review them and make sure that you have given some consideration to these five areas. In this way, regardless of your mission and strategic goals, your organization will be in a better position to succeed by meeting the primary objectives of any organization.

Creating Your First Objectives

Your next task is to take your first strategic goal and dissect it into the necessary tactical objectives required to fulfill the goal. It is important that you do not try to get too specific here; you are not listing jobs or tasks, but rather larger, or tactical, objectives. You should generally aim for two to five objectives per goal, although you may naturally have more or less than this.

It helps here to try to be as neutral or unbiased as possible in determining your objectives. Again, it is useful if you can brainstorm with someone who is business-wise but not chiropractic-savvy. Look at an example of this process.

Goal: To successfully treat our patients and restore their health to optimal levels

What objectives are required to fulfill this goal? (Hint: Try not to think like a chiropractor here.)

Well, for one thing, you would have to get patients to make appointments to schedule a visit with the doctor. Once they are in the office, you would have to provide a treatment program that restored their health to optimal levels (and a way to keep them coming in long enough for this to occur). This requires you to know what type of treatment is necessary and when you will know that optimal health is reached. Assuming optimal health refers to an ongoing process and not just a single point in time, then you would also need some sort of process or mechanism to review your patients periodically to determine if an intervention is required to maintain the optimal health state that they have reached.

Once you have dissected the goal in this way, you will begin to see specific areas to target with your objectives. In this example, there were three objectives:

1. Schedule patients effectively.
2. Provide a complete program of care.
3. Periodically review our patients' progress and provide a program of preventive maintenance care.

Note that these short statements are not overly descriptive. For example, scheduling patients requires a number of operations: having a trained CA, knowing how to answer the telephone, having an appointment book or computer-based system, having and furnishing an office, and so on. We will cover these specific tasks in the next chapter.

For now, we are the colonels trying to make sense of the strategic goals handed down to us by the general and trying to break each goal down into its basic and necessary components. This is tactical planning.

You will also note that each of the three objectives given in the above example would be amenable to objective measurement. Remember that this is the level of planning that primarily gives you your statistics.

Objective 1 (schedule patients effectively) could be measured by the number of office visits per week or month or the percentage of patients keeping their original appointments. Remember, at the tactical planning level, you only deal with part of the overall picture. You might wonder, for example, about new patients and where they are coming from. This would be the domain of a different goal. This goal is only about "successfully treating" and restoring health to optimal levels. It assumes that new patients will have been successfully attracted to the office. You see, when you have a complete set of goals and objectives, you can track, by statistics, which objectives are being met and which are not. Examples later in this chapter will illustrate this point in more detail.

Objective 2 (providing a complete program of care) could be measured by the number of patients who actually complete the program recommended to them. In practice, this is called the "patient visit average (PVA)" or "office visit average" (defined as the number of office visits divided by the number of new patients, usually measured monthly). If, for example, you determine that a complete program of care consists of 30 visits per year, and your patients average 28.9 visits per year, then you know that you are essentially meeting that objective. If your PVA is 12.3, then objective 2 is not being satisfied and this is where you need to look for solutions. As simple as this looks, many chiropractors constantly feel that if they just had more new patients, everything would be fine. Certainly, another set of objectives will deal with new patients, and no one would say that new patients are not important to a chiropractic practice. But the point is this: By using statistics to measure your objectives, you can pinpoint the problem and zoom in precisely where you need to take corrective action.

Objective 3 (periodically review our patient's progress and provide a program of preventive maintenance care) could be measured by the percentage and/or number of patients who are seen for progress examinations, and the percentage and/or number of patients who complete an annual program of care. There are no right or wrong answers here; you have to decide what it is that you are trying to achieve with an objective and what statistic would tell you whether or not you have succeeded.

Once you feel you have determined three or four objectives for your first goal, you must ask yourself this: How would someone know if I actually achieved each of these objectives? If the answer is not readily available from the wording of the objective, then you may have to rethink the objective. This is where an unbiased assistant is helpful.

Your first assignment is to dissect your first goal into its component objectives. Again, aim for three or four as a guideline, but if fewer or more fit the goal, that is acceptable.

EXERCISE 8

Write the tactical objectives that are necessary to fulfill your first strategic goal.

Goal 1 (from exercise 7):

Objectives:

How did you do?

When I am doing individual consulting with chiropractors, I find that they have difficulty with this step until they learn to detach from the bigger picture and try not to think like chiropractors for a moment. An unbiased observer usually does not have difficulty in determining objectives because they ask very simple questions:

- What, exactly, is the strategic goal?
- What three or four objective steps must be taken to achieve this goal?
- For each of the objectives, how would I know if I actually met the objective?
- Review your objectives in exercise 8 with these questions in mind. If necessary, modify your work until you are satisfied that your goal would be achieved if you successfully completed your stated objectives (each of which is measurable to an unbiased observer's satisfaction).

If you are happy with your responses, you should now review and assess your objectives using the seven characteristics of objectives discussed earlier in this chapter.

Make sure that you are satisfied that you meet these criteria. If not, review the wording of the objectives to get it right. If it seems impossible to do this, review the strategic goal. Perhaps you need to rework the goal before you can develop meaningful objectives. It is not uncommon to rework the entire process several times until you are happy with both the wording and the intent of the planning process.

Your next exercise is to write objectives and their measurable statistics for each of your strategic goals. Just to keep the process integrated in your mind, also include a re-write of the objectives in exercise 8. Please note that I have provided space on the following pages for five goals and five objectives for each goal. If you have fewer, no problem. If you have more, just use a separate piece of paper for your work. Having three to five goals and two to five objectives for each goal is only a guideline. It's your practice; you decide how many goals and objectives you need to fulfill your mission.

Take your time with this exercise. It is the vital link between your mission and the individual daily tasks necessary to fulfill it.

Chapter 5 Tactical Level Planning

EXERCISE 9

For each of your strategic goals, write the tactical objectives. For each objective, write the statistic that would best measure that objective.

Strategic Goal 1:

Objectives:

1.

2.

3.

4.

5.

Creating Your First Objectives **39**

Strategic Goal 2:

Objectives:

1.

2.

3.

4.

5.

Chapter 5 Tactical Level Planning

Strategic Goal 3:

Objectives:

1.

2.

3.

4.

5.

Strategic Goal 4:

Objectives:

1.

2.

3.

4.

5.

Chapter 5 Tactical Level Planning

Strategic Goal 2:

Objectives:

1.

2.

3.

4.

5.

Well done!

Using Statistics

Before we move to the chapter on operational level planning, I want to expand our exploration of statistics.

In an ideal world, each of your objectives (and you may have as few as 10 and as many as 25, if you followed the guidelines I have suggested) should be measurable and easily quantifiable.

But this is not an ideal world. Some areas simply do not allow for quantifiable measurement, and there is no point in creating a burdensome, artificial statistical process that will frustrate you. Remember that this process is not meant to be an albatross, but rather a valued assistant in managing your practice and steering it in the right direction.

Therefore, now that you are becoming an advanced student in the art and science of strategic planning, you are ready for your first ambiguity. What you may find is that in some areas, several qualitatively measurable objectives may collectively give rise to a quantitatively measurable goal. In other words, in some cases, the *strategic goal* may be the source of the measurable statistic, rather than the *tactical objective*.

Let me give you an example. Say that one of your goals is "to successfully manage our human resources and physical plant in order to support our mission." Now, just for a moment, envision yourself with a huge Mayo Clinic type of operation and imagine that you have assigned a manager to the department of human resources and physical plant.

This manager would oversee several objectives (in the above example, the doctor had four objectives for this goal), and these objectives would relate to areas such as the office itself (physical plant), the staff (office policies, training, and procedural manuals), and the process of making sure that the office and staff are capable of handling the patient flow. (Note that actually getting the patients into the clinic is another manager's goal area.) Each of these objectives would ideally have a specific measurement or statistic, but in reality, they all lead to one thing: the flow of patients through the office. In other words, this department manager's progress would ultimately be measured by the number of patients efficiently flowing through the clinic.

The four objectives were actually qualitative: either they were being done or they were not being done. But, as a collective group, they summated into an important function of the clinic: allowing for an efficient flow of a large number of patients. In other words, if the staff and physical plant are efficient enough and support the overall mission of serving "as many people as possible," then in reality, the best statistic is the collective statistic of "total office visits per month." In this case, you would have a statistic of the strategic goal, rather than a tactical objective.

Here is another example of a statistic derived from a goal rather than an objective. Your goal might be "to have a financially solvent practice which provides me with a stable professional income." This goal was broken down into three objectives that related to the fee schedule, the tracking of accounts receivable, and financial policies for patients. Certainly every objective was measurable, but only qualitatively. For example, either your fee schedule is current or it is not. Either you have a financial policy for patients or you do not. However, taken as a collective, this group of objectives yields a measurable monthly statistic: your total income from your practice. Three qualitative objectives summate to a quantitative statistic for your goal.

You should continue to aim for quantitative objectives, but as these examples show, you may find that the best statistics for your practice actually come from the goals rather than the objectives. Nonetheless, each objective must still be measurable and specific, for they are the foundations of your statistics, regardless of whether they are qualitative or quantitative.

Managing Complex Strategic Plans

One other variation of the process may help you with your strategic plan. Sometimes, due to the complexity of your plan, the lines get a little blurred between goals and objectives. In this case, another planning level called *divisions* may be helpful.

The following is an outline of a fairly complex strategic plan in which a larger-than-usual set of goals is grouped into three divisions (administrative, health-care delivery, and research and education). After you study the planning structure of this practice, decide for yourself: Are there really 10 goals within 3 divisions? Or, are there 3 goal areas with 10 objectives?

Ten goals are really quite a lot to handle unless you are a huge organization. However, you can simplify this effort without compromising the overall congruency of the plan and mission.

Using a divisional structure, you could divide the goals into naturally grouped areas. You could also create a divisional goal, rather than simply naming the divisions. What this does, in effect, is give you another slice in the planning pyramid, knocking everything down one rung.

In studying this example, you will find that the statistics shown are actually derived from the goals rather than the objectives. All the objectives were measurable and specific, but collectively, they provided a more meaningful set of statistics to measure the progress of the practice.

Managing Complex Strategic Plans

As long as you keep in mind the general principles of strategic planning, you should do what you can to keep your model as simple and organized as possible. If it seems more appropriate to add a divisional layer and derive the statistics from the goals rather than objectives, then go ahead.

Example

Vision

Our vision is universal access to high-quality chiropractic and natural health care.

Mission

Our mission and purpose is to adjust and educate as many people as possible toward optimal health through chiropractic and complementary natural health care.

Goals

Administrative Division

A. Office Management and Physical Plant

   Goal: To successfully manage and administer our office and physical plant in order to support our mission

   Statistic: Total office visits per month

B. Accounting

   Goal: To control costs and maximize revenue in order to provide resources for the survival and growth of the practice and staff

   Statistic: Fees charged and collected per month

C. Human Resources

   Goal: To successfully manage our human resources in order to support our mission

   Statistic: Staff turnover rate per year

D. Professional Sales and Supplies

   Goal: To sell products and supplies that complement our chiropractic practice

   Statistic: Net sales profits per month

Health-Care Delivery Division

E. Chiropractic Services

   Goal: To deliver the highest quality of chiropractic care to all patients

   Statistic: Patient visit average (PVA) per month

F. Complementary Health Services

   Goal: To deliver complementary natural healing methods, practices, and programs that support our mission

   Statistic: Nonchiropractic health services rendered per month

Research and Education Division
G. Public Education

> Goal: To identify and develop specific action plans to educate as many people as possible about chiropractic and as a result, to attract as many new patients as possible to our practice
>
> Statistic: Total new patients per month

H. Internal Education Program

> Goal: To develop patient education programs, as well as a passionate, charismatic atmosphere that will attract new patient referrals from our existing patients
>
> Statistic: Referred new patients per month

I. External Education Program

> Goal: To effectively promote the chiropractic story to the entire world, the result of which will be a constant supply of new patients
>
> Statistic: Nonreferred new patients per month

J. Research Program

> Goal: To develop an ongoing research agenda that supports the chiropractic profession as well as our mission
>
> Statistic: Number of papers published per year

This strategic outline may look more ambitious and complicated than you care to develop at this point in time, but look closely and you will see that it is not as complicated as it seems. Admittedly, you could eliminate goals D, F, and J, leaving you with 7 goal areas: still a bit larger than ideal. Goals G, H, and I could be amalgamated into 1 goal area, and this would then leave 5 goals, a reasonable number for a strategic plan. The problem is, this reduces the neatly packaged organization as it appears above into its bare bones. So take your choice: You either leave it as it is with 10 goals, but consolidate them into 3 divisions, or reduce the complexity so you have a more manageable plan.

There are no correct answers here. If you choose to leave the plan as it is with 10 goals, then by creating 3 divisions, you in effect create 3 goal areas. That way, the above-stated goals become objectives, and you can proceed from there into operational plans.

For your information, here are the numbers of objectives that were in the above example:

Goal A: 3 objectives
Goal B: 3 objectives
Goal C: 6 objectives
Goal D: 4 objectives
Goal E: 2 objectives

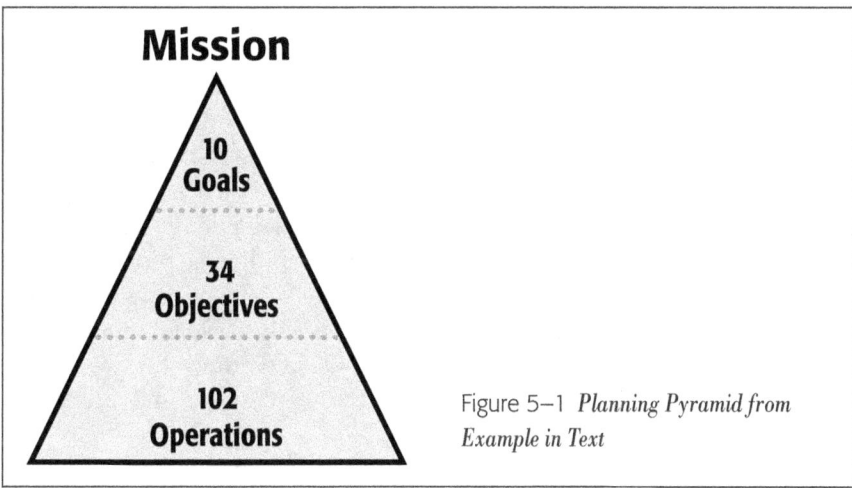

Figure 5–1 *Planning Pyramid from Example in Text*

Goal F: 1 objective
Goal G: 3 objectives
Goal H: 4 objectives
Goal I: 7 objectives
Goal J: 1 objective

You can see that from 10 goals were derived 34 objectives, from which were derived 102 operations. The planning pyramid is shown in **Figure 5–1**.

If we were to create 3 divisions, the resulting planning pyramid would look as shown in **Figure 5–2**.

The divisions could be in name only, as shown in the example, or they could actually be divisional goals. For example, "Administrative Division" could be

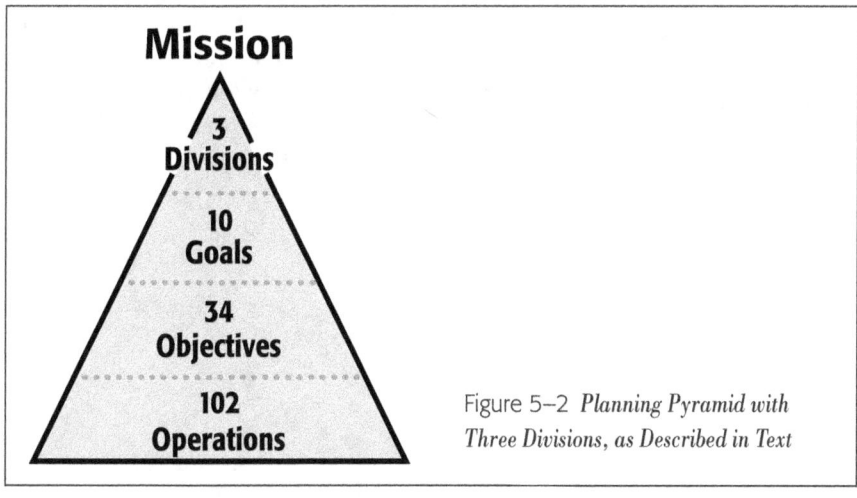

Figure 5–2 *Planning Pyramid with Three Divisions, as Described in Text*

replaced with "To provide administrative facilities and support for the clinical and educational goals of the practice."

You can see that you have some flexibility with the structure as long as the basic organizational plan is followed.

Note that in the plan as stated above, the area typically known as *marketing* is called *education*. Of course you can argue that this, too, is simply semantics, but I think there is a larger purpose to this selection of names. Your mission states that you aim to "educate" as many people as possible. If you develop your strategic plan from your mission statement, then "education" will necessarily be part of your goals. In fact, this is exactly what chiropractic marketing is (or should be): education of patients about chiropractic, health, and healing. Defining your goals in this way brings congruency and strength to your overall plan.

Before moving on to operational planning, I want to explain the numbering and lettering system we will be using. Your goals should be ordered using uppercase letters, as in A, B, C. Objectives should be numbered as subsets of goals, as in A1, A2, A3, B1, B2. Operational plans should be ordered with lowercase letters as subsets of objectives, as in A1a, A1b, A2a, A2b. You will find that further subdivision may be necessary when we get to day-to-day planning. Simply continue to follow the above conventions. For example, a subset of operational plans would be A1a1, A1a2, A1a3. This process is very important as you proceed since you will be managing a large number of operations and organization on paper as well as in your head is critical.

This would be a good time to review your plan up to this point. By now, you should have a written vision and mission statement. From this, you have derived up to five strategic goals, and each goal has been analyzed to identify up to five tactical objectives. Depending on how complex your mission is, you may have to interject a further planning layer called *divisions* to simplify your pyramid. In either case you should now have a number of measurable objectives for your practice. Our next job is to bring this process into the day-to-day operation of your clinic as we develop our operational plans.

> Make decisions based on desirable results, not desirable activities.
>
> —Dr. Michael Wiles

Chapter 6

Operational Level Planning

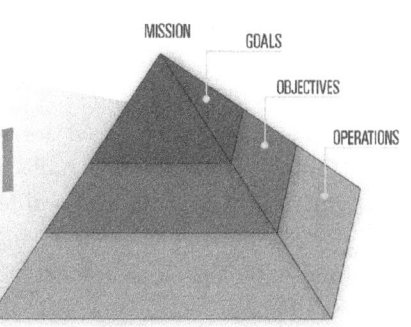

Operational level planning involves operating management, which is also called first-level management and is the lowest level of management. In the business world, operating supervisors must follow the tactical plans established by middle management to achieve the strategic goals formulated at the top. These are "the trenches" where the day-to-day work is done, translating what began with your vision, as a dream, into a reality.

> He who knows and does not act does not in fact know.
>
> —Buddha

The higher levels of planning, strategic and tactical, constitute *strategy formulation*. This lowest level, which includes plans, policies, procedures, and rules, constitutes *strategy implementation*.

Management consultants generally agree that the three managerial levels are not necessarily as clear-cut as we would like. Information in a large organization is constantly traveling from top to bottom and from bottom to top, and it is this exchange and feedback that help ensure that the entire organization constantly moves toward its goals.

For example, you may have a strategic goal to introduce or implement a new system of therapy or a new diagnostic technology. At the strategic level, the day-to-day implementation is somewhat uncertain. At the tactical level, you do your best to dissect the strategic goal into fundamental measurable objectives. Then you take each objective and work out the practical methods and plans for implementation. Only at that low level of operational planning may it become apparent that the goal is impractical, perhaps because of either time or money constraints. Accordingly, this information filters back up to the strategic level where some modification of the goals may be required. On the way up, middle management (or coordinating management) does its best to solve the problem by reallocating resources or reformulating tactical objectives.

This type of cybernetic management system occurs in large, well-run organizations all the time. The problem is, you happen to be the top, middle, and lower management levels of your practice. Therefore, be aware that as you work on the operational level, it may be necessary either to rework or rethink some of your tactics and, possibly, even your goals.

Translating Your Dream into Reality

This next section is perhaps somewhat tedious, but in reality it is the most crucial of the entire planning process. Planning does not create a successful practice, action does. Please keep this in mind. The translation of your dream into reality only occurs by *doing something*.

You must take the time to do this step carefully and review it to make sure that you have not missed anything. Some things will become obvious if they are accidentally omitted, but others will not, and you may find that you are not moving toward your goals simply because you omitted a key ingredient or step.

Think of yourself as writing the pilot's manual for flying a jet aircraft. Each required step must be included, or else! The flip side of this principle is economy of action. You cannot waste valuable time and resources on activities that do not have a direct and significant bearing on your tactical objectives. Waste or inefficiency have no place in your newly organized practice, and this is the planning level where you make sure that you have the most efficient plan in place.

As you work through these exercises to develop your operational plans, you will notice something interesting about plans. They are either "single-use" or "standing" plans. That is, they will have to be done only once (for example, buying an outdoor sign for the office) or they will be done with regularity—daily, weekly, monthly, or annually (for example, cleaning the office and paying your employees). Also, single-use plans can be subdivided into "programs" and "projects." Generally, programs involve the entire clinic's attention and resources (or, at least, the involvement of several interrelated areas), whereas a project is a subset of a program. Some management references consider a budget to be a third kind of single-use plan. Keep track of which plans are standing and which ones are single-use. Later you will use this information to create a critical action list and a prioritized list for single-use activities.

You will also notice that some plans of action will appear to be so critical to the operation of the clinic that you will define them as "rules." Examples of rules are the washing of hands before or after certain procedures, the wearing of name tags, or the use of titles and professional designations. You may wish to keep track of which items fall into this category so you can formulate a manual of rules or a manual of rules and regulations. Interestingly, the term *regulation* means "a rule of conduct," so in a sense, it is a redundancy. A regulation is simply a type of rule. A rule is defined as "a method or principle of action." Both words come from related Latin roots: regulation from *regulare*, meaning "to rule"; rule from *regula*, meaning "ruler." So you may feel free to call this collection of operational plans your Manual of Rules and Regulations.

Broader than a rule is a procedure. Procedures are plans that establish a customary method of handling future activities. Sometimes they are referred to as "standard operating procedures." They are narrower than policies, but broader than rules. Rules typically involve only a narrow segment of the overall strategic plan, procedures involve a larger segment such as an entire department, and policies are usually organizational in scope.

An example would be the procedure to follow for recall and reactivation of patients. Most chiropractors will have an action step that covers these procedures. The operational plan might be worded as "develop a routine method of recall and reactivation of inactive patients." This could actually be subdivided into two action steps: recall and reactivation. As the actual procedure is developed for these action steps, it is described in your strategic plan. Then this section becomes a part of your procedural manual, or manual of standard operating procedures.

You can see how important it is to develop your own procedural manual using this planning method. Many chiropractors purchase a procedural manual from a management group. While this is certainly better than nothing at all, it may lead to frustration because many parts of the manual will be either irrelevant or incongruent with your personal mission.

As you work through your tactical objectives one by one, identifying all the necessary tasks or operations, some may be customary methods of handling future activities. Keep track of these, because they will constitute your Procedural Manual.

Finally, as you proceed through the entire strategic planning process, you may develop or identify items that are "standing decisions intended to serve as overall guidelines to thinking and decision making." This is the management definition of policies. Policies may cut across planning levels and may be formulated at any level. They tend to be stable and can be specified in writing or developed out of common practice. An example would be your action step or operational plan dealing with overdue accounts, such as, "establish a firm policy regarding overdue accounts." As you identify these types of items, keep track of them, because they will constitute your policy manual.

Note that in the above examples, you are developing *action steps* in the operational level of planning. You still have another level of activity, which is the

Chapter 6 Operational Level Planning

execution, performance, or *doing* of these steps. As your strategic plan develops over the next few chapters, you will find that these action steps will tell you exactly what you must do to develop, run, and grow your practice. Policies, procedures, and rules will be developed only as necessary to help you move toward satisfying your mission. Yes, you have a lot of work to do yet, but the principle of economy of action is involved here as well. There will be no redundancies of activity, and you will be making decisions based on desirable results, not desirable activities.

When you look at the complexities involved in this process to keep it congruent with your mission and goals and to keep it relevant, you can see the importance of developing your own rules and regulations, procedures, and policies, rather than simply adopting someone else's.

To review briefly, by the time you identify all the tasks necessary to achieve your tactical objectives, you will find that they fall into several categories:

- Standing plans (done with regularity)
- Single-use plans (programs, projects, and budgets)
- Rules
- Procedures
- Policies

> The one thing that separates winners from losers is, winners take action!
> —Anthony Robbins

> When schemes are laid in advance, it is surprising how often circumstances fit in with them.
> —Sir William Osler

From these items you will construct three manuals of operation, a daily critical action list (also a monthly list and a yearly list), and a list of single-use plans that you will prioritize for completion over specified time periods. Sound good?

Here's a final word of advice on this subject: You may find it difficult to distinguish between operational items that would be best classified as rules and regulations, and those that would best be classified as operating procedures or policies. If this is the case, do not worry about it. As long as you identify items that are single-use and items that are standing (or repeatable), you are well on your way to a properly planned and operated practice. If necessary, simply collect all the standing plans into a manual of rules, procedures, and policies. Call it what you like, as long as you understand that you are listing the critical action steps that are necessary to operate your practice successfully and achieve your overall strategic mission.

Creating Your Operational Plans

As far as the hard work goes, you are now over the hump. This next stage is tedious, however, and it may take some time. But remember how important this is. You may not be creating a manual for flying a jet, but you are creating a plan for your personal and professional survival and growth. Take it seriously, and you will be justly rewarded by the achievement of your goals. What greater reward for the hard work can there be than seeing your mission and vision fulfilled in your lifetime? If this does not create a bodily stir of emotion, then you may have to go back and rework your vision!

The next exercise is so important that I am taking some extra time to go over exactly what is required. As you take each tactical objective and dissect it into its necessary action steps, you may find that some of them easily, painlessly, and quickly yield up their operational plans.

> With a definite, step-by-step plan—ah, what a difference it makes! You cannot fail, because each step carries you along to the next, like a track.
>
> —*Scott Reed*

Example

A3 To have an effective physical plant to support our mission

    A3a Ensure that office is visible via appropriate signs. (*Single-use plan*)

    A3b Create a noteworthy and educational reception room through decoration and accessories. (*Policy*)

    A3c Ensure a fully functional and clean reception desk and work area at all times. (*Procedure*)

    A3d Establish specific room functions and names (for example, examination room, adjustment room, patient education center). (*Policy*)

    A3e Fully furnish and equip the office as necessary to support the mission. (*Single-use plan*)

    A3f Establish routine method of physical plant review and identify standards by which the physical plant may be maintained (for example, no equipment left on floor, no dirty gowns left in rooms, diagnostic equipment spotlessly clean and sterile, adjusting table upholstery intact) (*Standing plan: office maintenance schedule and standards*; *policy: cleanliness and standards*).

These items are relatively straightforward. You may, of course, have thought of others to include, but you get the idea that the construction of operational plans is sometimes fairly easy.

However, sometimes this is not the case, and then you can use the following five-step process for formulating operational plans. Ideally you should apply this process to every objective, but in practice and in reality you may only have to apply it where ambiguity or difficulty arises in determining the exact course of action to achieve a given objective.

Step 1 is the identification of the objective. You completed this step in the previous chapter.

Step 2 is to identify the key elements of the objective. This is similar to the exercise in which you broke down each goal into component parts from which you derived your objectives. You can do the same thing for operational tasks. Simply apply an unbiased brainstorming process to each objective and ask yourself the question: What, exactly, would have to be done to achieve this particular objective?

Step 3 is to develop scenarios on paper to estimate the impact of different actions you might take to achieve the objective. Perhaps one scenario involves the purchase of equipment, whereas another scenario to achieve the very same objective involves the hiring of additional personnel. Think each one out carefully before committing to a final response. Remember the military example of D-day. You might decide, as sergeant, that you could approach the enemy bunker from the north, with such-and-such likely casualties, or from the south, with such-and-such likely outcome. You have to make a judgment call for each item, and time will tell which is correct. But at least you have taken the time to explore alternative future scenarios. (Remember the quote at the front of the book: "Dig the well before you thirst.")

Step 4 is to choose the best scenario from your alternative scenarios.

Step 5 is to determine if this course of action is congruent with your existing rules, procedures, and policies; if it creates any new rules, procedures, and policies; and to ensure that it is not in conflict with any other plans.

You are now at the point where you must develop your action steps, or operational plans, from your objectives.

Take each objective individually and brainstorm to determine the necessary, but minimum, action steps required to achieve the objective. Think like a manager determining the exact action steps that your floor supervisor will give to your plant workers. Nothing more, nothing less.

As you develop these action steps, be sure to list them properly using the numbering and lettering scheme I have described. Also, keep track of which items might reasonably be considered rules, procedures, and policies, as well as which items are standing plans and which are single-use plans. (Please note that most, but not all, standing plans will fall into the categories of rules, procedures, or policies. Some are simply unclassified action steps that must be done with regularity to operate the practice.) This information is valuable in the next series of steps you will take with your strategic plan.

Finally, avoid the temptation of being drawn into actually *doing* the action steps at this point. As you come across items such as "develop a logo for use on all office stationery and forms," or "develop and utilize a routine method of recall and reactivation of inactive patients," it may seem tempting to actually develop these items as they come to mind. Perhaps you have information necessary to the development of these items, and you are afraid of losing it or the ideas that are coming out of the planning process. This is natural. The way around it is to have file folders with the item name and number so that any resource material you happen to come across can be immediately put in the appropriate folder for future action.

Organizing Your Plans

It is an excellent idea, in fact, to have a numbered file folder for each action item, even if there is nothing to put in the folder at this point in time. Now that you are becoming organized, you will find it easier to stay organized and also to be able to keep better control of all actions in your practice (remember, you are the CEO).

Many of you will wish to keep your information on your computer, and your file folders will actually be electronic file folders. Obviously, do what is best for you and your practice, and what you are comfortable doing. However, my advice is to keep a hard copy file of this information as well.

Somehow, organization becomes more recognizable when you can actually see the paper with the plan or action steps on it. Also, the resources that you collect for some items may be newspaper clippings, catalogs, order forms, photocopied forms, or articles, and ultimately you will have to be able to organize all this material and make it easily retrievable.

Ideally, you should have a filing cabinet with an executive folder containing a copy of the entire strategic plan and your list of critical daily action steps (more on this later); your manuals of rules, procedures, and policies; and files numbered and named as I have described. If you do this, you will literally have the entire planning process at your fingertips at all times. When you unexpectedly come across some item or information that might help you with one of your operations, you will be able to place it exactly where it should be filed for future use. I know this sounds easy and obvious, but you would be surprised at the number of doctors who neglect a straightforward system of filing and storage of information.

Use the following pages to list your action steps based on your objectives. Since I do not know how many goals or objectives you have, I cannot provide an exact framework for you, so simply use the structure suggested. For your reference, and as a guide, I have reproduced a template for the strategic plan in **Appendix 3**.

Exercise 10

List your operational plans using the following structural format and numbering system.

Example

> Goal B: To control costs and maximize revenue in order to provide resources for the survival and growth of the practice and staff
>
> Objective B1: To maintain an efficient and effective fee schedule and collection system designed to minimize accounts receivable
>
>> Operational Plan B1a: Establish a fee schedule for all services rendered and a catalog of services and products sold [policy].
>>
>> Operational Plan B1b: Establish, as part of an overall fee schedule, special fees for unique groups [single-use plan leading to policies].
>>
>>> Operational Plan B1b1: Establish a "company chiropractor" fee schedule [policy].
>>>
>>> Operational Plan B1b2: Establish criteria and fixed fees for charity cases [policy].
>>>
>>> Operational Plan B1b3: Establish special fees for entire families [policy].
>>
>> Operational Plan B1c: Establish firm front-desk procedures and control methods for collecting fees [procedure].
>>
>>> Operational Plan B1c1: Develop a "financial consultation" performed by the CA at the patient's report of findings [procedure].
>>>
>>> Operational Plan B1c2: Develop specific procedures to follow at front desk for routine visits, new patients, and reactivated patients with regard to collecting fees [procedure].
>>
>> Operational Plan B1d: Establish firm policy regarding the handling of overdue accounts [policy].
>
> Objective B2: To keep our fee schedule current and to review fees in order to effectively charge for all services rendered
>
>> Operational Plan B2a: Perform an annual fee review of local chiropractors and other health providers [procedure].
>>
>> Operational Plan B2b: Perform an annual review of all fees, services, and financial policies [procedure].
>>
>> Operational Plan B2c: Perform an annual review of office expenses to maximize profit and to minimize overhead [procedure].
>
> Objective B3: (etc.)

Organizing Your Plans **57**

Use the following six pages to develop your own set of operational plans as directed.

Operational Plans

Act well at the moment and you have performed a great action for all eternity.
—Johann Kaspar Lavater (1741–1801)

Chapter 6 Operational Level Planning

Operational plans (continued)

> Leadership is action, not position.
> —*Donald McGannon*

Operational plans (continued)

> For purposes of action, nothing is more useful than narrowness of thought combined with energy of will.
>
> —*Henri Frederic Amiel*

Chapter 6 Operational Level Planning

Operational plans (continued)

> And do it now. There may be a law against it tomorrow.
> —*Lawrence J. Peters*

Operational plans (continued)

> As life is action and passion, it is required of man that he should share the action and passion of his time, at peril of being judged not to have lived.
>
> —*Oliver Wendell Holmes, Jr.*

Chapter 6 Operational Level Planning

Operational plans (continued)

The great end of life is not knowledge, but action.
—*Thomas Huxley (1825–1895)*

Chapter 7

Doing First
Things First

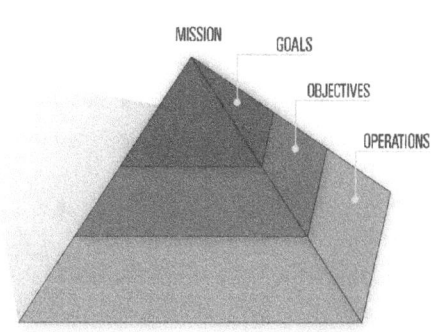

At this point in your planning journey, you have a vision, a mission, a set of strategic goals derived from the mission, and a set of tactical objectives derived from each goal. Finally, you derived a set of operational plans from your list of objectives. These plans are divided into plans that you do only once (single-use plans) and those that require repetitive action (standing plans). Many, if not most, of your standing plans can be further divided into items that fall into the categories of rules (and regulations), procedures, and policies.

> It takes twenty years to make an overnight success.
> —Eddie Cantor

What do you do with all this information? You may have your own ideas on this subject. In that case, I wish you luck and success as you proceed to action steps based on your new strategic plan. On the other hand, I suspect that most practice planners will need some further guidance as they turn this grand scheme into scheduled action steps.

There are basically two approaches you can take: prioritization based on either tactical objectives or operational tasks. The former is the preferred method for an established practice, and the latter is ideally suited for the new practice. Let me explain.

If you have an established practice and you are embarking on a planning process to revitalize your practice or to embrace a new format, technique, or style of practice, then you have a double challenge because you have to make changes in vivo. Most commonly, you will retain many of your operational activities in your new plan. That is, you rarely discard all the operating functions and principles that you have developed during the life of your practice. Instead, the strategic level (your overall direction in practice) has changed, and it is at the tactical level that these changes are most evident. New tactical objectives are de rigueur in a new strategic plan, and this intermediate level of planning has to blend the new, revitalized practice with the existing operation as it continues on a day-to-day basis. In other words, changing tires while the car is in motion requires careful coordination of the strategic and operational levels, which is exactly the task of middle-level management, or tactical planning.

On the other hand, if your practice is brand-new, or in the event that you have an opportunity to start again completely (for example, after a lengthy practice interruption or after a significant location change to a different state or country), then you can literally build afresh from the bottom-up (after planning afresh from above-down!). In this case, it is the operational tasks that can be prioritized and executed according to what is critically important to getting you up and running as quickly as possible.

Execution Plan A–Tactical Prioritization
(Recommended for existing and established practices)

As an established chiropractor, your first priority is to keep the practice running and solvent, while you make crucial changes. This is an interesting challenge and keeping focused and organized is obviously very important. Also, you are likely to have other team members whose input is valuable in the planning process, so you will need their support and participation.

Let me just say a quick word about teamwork since it is so important at this planning stage. In management, the theory and practice of decision making (and group decision making) are lofty and detailed subjects, beyond the scope of this text. However, here are some basic concepts for you to keep in mind as you proceed with your plans.

You need to look at two "tests" to determine whether a team member should participate in the decision-making process. Is the issue relevant to that team member? And does that team member have the necessary expertise to render a decision? Consider the matrix shown in **Table 7-1**.

Type I decisions involve team members and subordinates as early as possible in the decision-making process. In Type II decisions, the main purpose of involvement of the team member is to communicate the rationale for the decision and to lower resistance to the decision. In Type III decisions, the team member is involved to improve the decision-making process, and in both Types II and III, it is made clear to the team member that the final decision will be

Table 7–1 *Types of Decisions*

Test of relevance	Yes	Yes	No	No
Test of expertise	Yes	No	Yes	No
Member involvement	Frequent	Occasionally	Occasionally	Never
Type of decision	I	II	III	IV

made by you, the doctor. Type IV decisions are purely administrative decisions that do not involve the team members at all.

Trying to use this matrix in a strict fashion will lead to frustration, so just use it as a guideline. In any event, you, the doctor, will make the final decisions in your practice. Unfortunately, since you are trained as a health professional and not as an administrator, stress can arise from either overusing subordinates in the decision-making process (which leads to stress for them too) or underutilizing them (which can lead to frustration and resentment). Try to recognize their needs and expertise levels appropriately, and you will gain their support and enthusiasm for the strategic process.

Notwithstanding the previous information about shared decision making, your next exercise can be done by yourself, with a trusted associate, or with your entire team in a democratic fashion. As a chief executive, you are not bound to act on the majority will, but you may wish to try the democratic method. Let me tell you how this method works and give you an example.

In a perfect world, you would like every job on your list done tomorrow (or today, for that matter). However, if you have just assembled a list of more than 100 practical jobs to perform, this is simply not going to happen. You should first determine a reasonable time period to complete the jobs, culminating in a planning retreat for yourself (and perhaps your team) so you can review your entire plan again. This could be a 6-month plan or a 1-, 2-, or 3-year plan.

Next, you should prioritize the tactical objectives. Write each objective on a card or piece of paper and have each team member place the items in the order of relative importance from first to last. Obviously this is not easy because properly determined objectives are all important. You must decide, however, where to put your energies first and foremost. Force yourself to decide what is the absolutely most important area to pursue first. Then, having removed that item from the list, force yourself to choose the most important item from the remainder, and so on.

Here is an example of this process using a grading scale. Each practice team member assigned a number to each objective, with the most important item being number 1. In this example, 14 objectives were categorized as follows:

A1, A2, and A3 were related to patient scheduling and treatment

Goal A: To successfully treat our patients and restore their health to optimal levels

    A1: To use effective and efficient communication and appointment scheduling procedures

    A2: To provide a complete program of chiropractic care

    A3: To periodically review our patients' progress and provide a program of preventive care

B1, B2, B3, and B4 were related to patient education

Goal B: To educate our patients and the public about chiropractic

    B1: To have a clean and aesthetic office that comforts and educates

    B2: To give seminars and lectures to our patients

    B3: To utilize an organized patient education program

    B4: To develop a public education system

C1, C2, and C3 were related to community outreach and marketing

Goal C: To serve the health needs of the community

    C1: To develop a program of health and chiropractic promotion

    C2: To instill a referral consciousness in our patients

    C3: To study and respond to community health concerns

D1, D2, D3, and D4 were related to practice finances and solvency

Goal D: To provide sufficient resources for the survival and growth of the practice and staff

    D1: To develop and utilize an efficient fee collection system

    D2: To keep our fee schedule current and effectively charge for all services rendered

    D3: To decrease overhead and maximize resources wherever possible

    D4: To develop feedback systems to maximize office productivity

The average scores of these 14 objectives (averaged from five practice team members, with 1 being most important and 14 being considered the least important), are shown in **Table 7-2**. If a practice team member thought that a particular objective was really, really important and deserved to be tackled before anything else, it was given a score of 1. Each practice team member, therefore, placed the 14 objectives in order of importance from number 1 to number 14.

In this case, the doctor decided on a 3-year plan to revitalize his 14-year-old practice. Studying the above scores, three populations of results emerged: scores of 1 to 6, 7 to 10, and 10 to 14.

The reassembling of these data into a 3-year priority schedule is shown in **Table 7-3**.

Table 7-2 *Scoring of Objectives for Importance*

A1	5.8	B1	4.4	C1	10.2	D1	5.2
A2	3.8	B2	7.2	C2	5.4	D2	4.2
A3	7.4	B3	8.0	C3	9.0	D3	12.0
		B4	11.4			D4	11.0

Interestingly, the various staff members' scores for these yearly groupings were closely correlated (see **Table 7–4**) with only two exceptions (indicated with asterisks).

With these results in mind, a 3-year plan was created as follows:

Year 1: A1, A2, B1, C2, D1, D2
Year 2: A3, B2, B3, C3
Year 3: B4, C1, D3, D4

Now obviously, this doctor could not just stop practicing for 3 years while this plan was implemented. Life goes on, and so does practice. However, the general plan for the next 3 years was plotted out.

Complete the following exercise, either alone or with your staff (or both), and determine your objective priorities for the future. Note that, at this point, we are not yet concerned with whether items are single-use plans or standing plans; we are simply looking at tactical objectives (not operational plans).

Table 7-3 *Three-Year Priority Schedule*

Objective	Year 1	Year 2	Year 3	Goal Category
A1	5.8			Scheduling and treatment
A2	3.8			Scheduling and treatment
A3		7.4		Scheduling and treatment
B1	4.4			Patient education
B2		7.2		Patient education
B3		8.0		Patient education
B4			11.4	Patient education
C1			10.2	Community outreach
C2	5.4			Community outreach
C3		9.0		Community outreach
D1	5.2			Practice solvency
D2	4.2			Practice solvency
D3			12.0	Practice solvency
D4			11.0	Practice solvency
Average	4.8	7.9	11.2	

Table 7-4 *Average Ranking Scores of 14 Objectives by Practice Team Members*

	Year 1	Year 2	Year 3
Doctor-owner	4.0	7.8	12.5
Doctor-associate	5.3	9.5	8.8*
Doctor-associate	7.2	3.5*	12
Chiropractic assistant	3.5	8.8	12.3
Chiropractic assistant	4.0	10.0	10.3
Average	4.8	7.9	11.2

* Average rankings for these doctors did not correlate well with those assigned by other team members.

Exercise 11

Determine your time limits for your strategic plan and prioritize your objectives within these time constraints.

(Hint: Depending on the size of your plan, you should be thinking about a minimum of 6 months and a maximum of 5 years for completion. If your time choice is inappropriate, you will discover it in one of the next exercises, at which point you can return to this exercise and do it over again.)

A man who dares to waste one hour of time has not discovered the value of life.

—*Charles Darwin*

At this point, you have to make a judgment call: Determine your ideal time frame for the first phase of your strategic plan. In the above example, which was a 3-year plan, each smaller phase was 1 year. You may have a 6-month plan with 1-month intervals or a 2-year plan with quarterly intervals or a 3-year plan with yearly intervals. Only you can decide how fast you want to be there and how much you can reasonably squeeze into your time and yet still be effective in all your current tasks and responsibilities.

If you cannot decide, choose a 3-year plan with yearly intervals or a 2-year plan with 6-month intervals.

Exercise 12

Determine your first *time interval, and list the objectives to be accomplished within that time frame.*
(Example: 12-month period; objectives A1, A2, B1, C2, D1, D2)

At this point, it is important to note that we are going to concentrate on this shorter time period only. Near the end of this time period, you will take some time to repeat this exercise and the following exercise to determine which objectives you will work on next. But for now, we are putting our whole effort into the task at hand; first things first!

As the chief executive of your practice, you have created the grand strategic plan. By constantly reviewing it, from the top-down, you function as the plan's protector and defender. This becomes very important when you and your staff begin to focus on (sometimes, extremely) narrow operational tasks. It is very easy, as the old saying goes, to lose track of the fact that you are there to drain the swamp when you are up to your backside in alligators. But since you have carefully created the master plan, and since you review it constantly for relevance and congruence, and since you have scheduled a complete review of the entire planning process (at least annually), then you can relax and know that the master plan is safe and secure and that you can fully concentrate on the operational tasks without becoming sidetracked.

It is a good idea at this point to create a priority planning document, not only for yourself, but as a point of agreement and clarification with your staff. After all, you want total cooperation for this plan to work.

Using the previous example (on page 66), the following document was created and distributed:

Year 1 Program

1. *Develop scheduling procedures, office manual, new patient protocol, recall and appointment procedures (A1).*
2. *Provide complete program of care: initial (symptom), corrective, and maintenance (A2).*
3. *Plan clean, aesthetic office that comforts and educates (B1).*
4. *Instill a referral consciousness in our patients (make them excited and enthusiastic) that involves our attitudes as much as our actions (C2).*
5. *Develop and use an efficient collection system (D1).*
6. *Keep our fee schedule current and effectively charge for all services rendered; develop a catalog of services for use in reception room (D2).*

You have come a long way from the creation of a vision statement. As you worked down from the vision statement and through the strategic, tactical, and operational levels, the planning pyramid became wider and wider. Now, to make your job feasible, we are dividing the final level of the pyramid into smaller and smaller time periods.

Just as you divided your overall plan into yearly, semiyearly, or quarterly chunks, you now have to divide your first block into smaller time periods. This final division of time should leave you with periods of 1 to 2 months only. (While this is only a guideline, you would be advised to try to limit your final planning periods to somewhere between a minimum of 1 month and a maximum of 3 months.)

Hang in there; you are coming up to your final exercises. Your next job is to list all the operational plans for the objectives you selected in your first planning period; we will call them first-period objectives. Just so you understand: In the previous example (see page 67), the first planning period is 1 year and the first-period objectives are A1, A2, B1, C2, D1, and D2.

In the example given, 46 operational tasks were associated with these 6 objectives. These 46 tasks were written on cards and distributed to the practice team and divided into 6 priority groupings covering six 2-month periods. The doctor then created his own priority lists within each of these 2-month periods. Since the staff members had all participated in this decision-making process, they had a high degree of loyalty to the overall strategic plan.

Exercise 13

Subdivide your first time period into smaller chunks (suggestion: 1 to 2 months each), and distribute all the operational tasks associated with your first-period objectives into these smaller time periods. If possible, get your staff to participate in this process.

Chapter 7 Doing First Things First

In the example given on pages 66–68, this exercise was completed as follows:
Months 1 to 2: A1a, A1c, A1g, A1h, B1d, D1b, D2b, D2d
Months 3 to 4: A1b, A2f, A2j, C2c, C2f, C2g, D1a, D2a
Months 5 to 6: A2a, A2b, A2c, A2e, A2i, B1a, D2c
Months 7 to 8: A2h, A2m, B1c, B1g, C2a, C2e, C2h, D1c
Months 9 to 10: A1d, A1e, A1f, A1i, A2g, A2l, B1e
Months 11 to 12: A2d, A2k, B1b, B1f, C2b, C2d, D1d, D1e
(Also included in month 12 was a planning session to develop the year 2 schedule, covering objectives A3, B2, B3, and C3)

Note that the 46 operational plans are about evenly distributed among the six, 2-month periods. Obviously, all the items are not equal in terms of the work necessary for their completion, but overall, groupings of seven or eight tasks average out to similar workloads. Make every effort to ensure a consistent workload throughout your subdivided time periods.

Your final task is to create a planning document for each of your subdivided time periods, outlining the tasks to be completed and the person or persons responsible for their completion.

Our example, with two, 2-month periods, is shown in **Table 7–5**.

As these jobs are scheduled, assigned, and completed, you will begin to accumulate rules and regulations, procedures, and policies that you have created, out of necessity, to comply with your overall strategic plan. Collect these documents in the appropriate binders or booklets. Over time, you will assemble a set of operating documents that will provide for stability and reference as your practice evolves and grows.

> Concentrate upon the work at hand. The sun's rays do not burn until brought to a focus. Work will win when wishing won't.
>
> — Dr. BJ Palmer

Finally, it is a good idea to date and number these documents as they are produced. In this way you can refer to them quickly through an index, and you can tell at a glance when the item was created (example: Fee Policy, version 1, September 2007).

From here, proceed to Chapter 8 on page 81.

Execution Plan B—Operational Prioritization
(Recommended for New Practices)

New graduates and doctors who are starting brand-new practices have a unique advantage because they can launch their new practice after a suitable planning

Table 7–5 *Example of Planning Document for Two, 2-Month Periods*

June–July (tasks to be completed by July 31)

A1a: Use proper and effective telephone technique.

A1c: Use effective "closing techniques" when speaking with potential patients.

A1g: Instill in patients the need to keep their appointments and follow through with recommended care.

A1h: Refine and develop effective new patient procedure, including a formal new-patient package.

B1d: Make sure our office is visible to the public via appropriate signs.

D1b: Establish a firm front desk financial policy and control methods.

D2b: Establish an annual review date for reviewing all services and fees; perform a fee review of local chiropractic offices.

D2d: Establish a special fee structure and company chiropractor program for local industries.

August–September (tasks to be completed by September 30)

A1b: Select and implement use of appropriate patient-scheduling software and/or appointment book.

A2f: Develop and use motivational material to keep patients enthusiastic and interested in their care.

A2j: Develop and use a thorough history/examination format for new patients (including the development of a new-patient kit).

C2c: Conduct a referral source analysis and develop a plan to increase referrals.

C2f: Develop an ongoing staff training program focusing on regular patient procedures, new patient procedures, and referral motivation.

C2g: Develop specific methods for immediately and effectively acknowledging all referrals; establish method for recording and tracking all new patient and referral sources.

D1a: Offer to accept Visa, MasterCard, Amex, and debit cards as methods of payment.

D2a: Establish a fee schedule for all services rendered and a catalog of all products sold.

---

period. Obviously, you want to get going as soon as possible, so this planning period should be kept to a minimum. Nevertheless, you have a unique opportunity to create a blueprint and build from the ground up.

If you have completed exercises 1 through 10*, you have a complete list of all the operational tasks necessary to execute your grand strategic plan. You are now faced with the task of prioritizing these tasks. At this point, most doctors are afraid that they will not prioritize properly and that this will adversely affect their practice development. Obviously, to some extent, this is a valid concern, and the following guidelines will help alleviate this issue. On the other hand, midstream corrections are not only possible but inevitable. Don't worry—just get to work—eventually it all gets done anyway!

As a first step in the prioritization process, you have to identify each item on your operational list as a standing plan or a single-use plan. You should have done this in exercise 10 (page 56). If you have not actually labeled each operational step as requested, please go back and make sure that your operations are clear, numbered, and identified as to their type.

Next, you must separate the single-use plans from the standing plans and, at the same time, separate your standing plans into rules, procedures, policies, and "other" (items that do not readily fall into the other categories). Do not try to prioritize the items yet; simply separate them into their respective categories. This initial segregation of your items is very important, because we will treat each category differently in the next series of exercises. On the next two pages, complete this re-organization exercise, listing your various operational plans and tasks in the appropriate categories.

Exercise 14
From your list of operational tasks (exercise 10), create a list of all your single-use plans:

---

*Exercises 11 through 13 relate to Execution Plan A.

Execution Plan B—Operational Prioritization

(More space may be required—use separate sheets as necessary.)

Chapter 7 Doing First Things First

Exercise 15

From your list of operational tasks (exercise 10), create a list of all your standing plans, and categorize them as you are able into rules and regulations, procedures, and policies. Refer to pages 50–52 as necessary for assistance.

(More space may be required—use separate sheets as necessary.)

Start with your list of single-use plans. If you recall from the initial description of these plans, they can also be subdivided into programs and projects, depending on their scope and whether they involve a small, isolated section of the practice (projects) or larger, integrated sections of the practice (programs). It is not necessary to subdivide your single-use plans this way as long as you realize that some are necessarily of greater scope than others.

You now have a list of anywhere from 20 to 120 items on your page, and your next task is to do your best to prioritize them from the most critical items downward. If you are a new graduate, you are likely doing this exercise on your own, which is quite alright. However, if you are able to enlist the aid of another person (ideally a business-savvy person), you may find the second opinion refreshing and helpful.

I recommend that you write each item on a card or piece of paper so you can physically move it around on a table surface. Now ask yourself: What is the single most important item necessary for me to start practice? This is definitely not an easy process. To ease your anxiety, here is a secret: there is no right or wrong way to do this. You will be doing a lot of work in a short time, so whether a particular item is number 3 or number 33 is not critical, as long as it is not number 103, if you deem it an important task.

Once you have this prioritized list of critical tasks, you must subdivide it into discrete time periods. How long do you want it to be before your practice is up and running at full speed? Obviously, "not very long" is the correct answer. However, building a successful practice does take time. Be realistic and determine a time frame within which you will complete your list of tasks. Can you do it in 12 months or 6 months or 3 months?

Once you have determined the time frame for your plan, you must break up your items into smaller, discrete chunks. For example, if you have 90 single-use plans and you wish to complete these tasks over a 1-year period, you may wish to divide your plan into six, 2-month periods of 15 tasks each. The length of the time periods is totally up to you and your anticipated energy in completing these tasks; just be realistic. It is natural to make corrections to both the list and time periods once you get started, but you want to keep such corrections to a minimum.

Chapter 7 Doing First Things First

Exercise 16

Prioritize your single-use plans from most important to least important, and determine a time frame for completion of these plans (usually between 6 months and 3 years). Finally, subdivide your list into smaller working time periods (usually between 1 and 3 months each). Your list should be roughly evenly distributed among these time periods. This list is called your list of programs and projects.

DC = Discipline + Consistency

—*Dr. Michael Wiles*

Next, we have to do something similar with your standing plans (from exercise 15). In this case, you should divide up the items according to their frequency of performance as well as according to their nature as rules and regulations, procedures, and policies.

To get started with the next exercise, create a document that includes all of these items. You can call this document your manual of standard operating procedures. I would suggest that you prepare this document as a three-ring binder, complete with a cover page and an index. Your collection of rules and regulations and your policies can be included as separate sections or as appendices to the main document. The key thing is that you have assembled this document independently and based on your actual needs as a chiropractor. It should be complete and relevant. Any deficiencies (and you will discover them) will become apparent as your plan is executed. At such times, you simply amend your plan, inform your staff, and insert the new information into your binder.

One more important point: At this time, you may simply have a title for some or most of these items. You cannot be expected to have every one of these operational plans completed at the beginning of this process. Some critical items will have to be completed immediately, but others can be scheduled for completion later. In that case, simply insert a page into your binder containing only the name and number of the item to be scheduled for completion.

Exercise 17

Obtain a three-ring binder (or reasonable substitute), and create a manual of standard operating procedures, as described above.

Now you have a prioritized list of single-use plans for implementation over a specified time period, as well as a binder of standard operating procedures, rules, and policies. Next we have to create a daily action checklist to schedule the completion of these items as you operate your practice.

From here, proceed to Chapter 8 on page 81.

Chapter 8

Daily Critical Action Steps

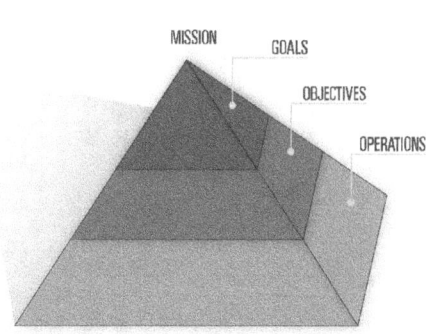

One of the most important aspects of any planning process is accountability. As the doctor, this may be even more difficult because you are accountable to yourself. Disciplined and consistent action is required, however, for your plan to become a reality.

I think that one of the best ways to do this is to create a list of daily critical action steps (also called a list of critical daily action steps). From your list of standing plans (procedures, rules, and policies), you must extract those

> Whatever failures I have known, whatever errors I have committed, whatever follies I have witnessed in private or public life have been the consequence of action without thought.
>
> —Bernard Baruch

jobs that have to be done on a daily or a weekly basis. This list may contain, for example, tasks like keeping up-to-date with insurance reports and documentation, phoning new patients after their first adjustment, reviewing the physical plant for cleanliness and supplies, checking inventory, reviewing accounts receivable, and reading your vision and mission (preferably aloud).

You will be creating a checklist to complete each day, guaranteeing that no task will be overlooked. After that, it is up to you to do the work or delegate it. Ultimately it is you who is responsible for the completion of the tasks and, therefore, your own success. So take this step seriously and remember: DC stands for discipline and consistency.

Add to this list any personal items that you feel are important to do on a daily or weekly basis, even though they may not have explicitly originated from your strategic plan. For example, a daily exercise routine or a daily meditation ritual may be on your list, as well as reading motivational material. You could, of course, add almost anything here (like take out the trash and pick up the groceries), but I would strongly suggest that you include only professional activities or those that directly affect your practice or your ability to practice.

Once this is done, you will create a chart to use every day. Quite frankly, if you get nothing else out of this book, this one exercise is worth a tremendous amount as a method of keeping you focused on your practice and on critical tasks.

Exercise 18

Make a list of all daily and weekly action steps, from your standing plans only. Add any other important daily or weekly tasks of a personal nature that affect your professional practice but may not have been forthcoming from your strategic planning process.

Now, think about the list you have created. By doing these tasks, you will be steadily moving to the completion of your strategic plan, right?

Partly right...

You need to include a number of other items. For example, if you have not added "read your vision, mission, and goals" as a daily task, please do so. Reviewing your plan daily is definitely a critical act for success. Also, what about your single-use plans (your list of programs and projects)?

You must add an item called "scheduled programs and projects" as a daily action step. Personally, I would also add "inspirational reading" as a daily task, as well as "exercise," which is a critical step because you cannot perform the physical rigors of chiropractic practice without being in shape yourself. Have you considered a "continuing education program"? Is this a step that was naturally forthcoming from your strategic plan? If not, you may want to review your plan to see if this has any official place in it; otherwise, consider it as a daily action step toward improving your professional knowledge and competence.

Finally, whatever else is on your list, add "weekly staff meeting," "prepare for next day," and "prepractice briefing." Many chiropractors completely neglect a weekly staff meeting, and many others hold a meeting but do not really know why. Your meetings can include a training session for you and your staff to develop various situational scenarios and practice your procedures (for example, what do you do if a patient has a medical emergency in the office? What do you do if a patient becomes belligerent? How do you handle an emergency walk-in during a busy time?). More importantly, though, your meetings should be a time to sit back and review the overall strategic plan and to take corrective action as necessary to keep the plan moving successfully forward. For example, an item may not be completed because of staff conflict, lack of materials, or lack of motivation, among other reasons.

Your weekly staff meeting can provide a forum for the identification and resolution of these types of problems. Do not discuss personal concerns with specific staff members in a weekly staff meeting. Meetings should be no longer than one hour in length (preferably shorter), and you may feel the need to have two separate times for the office meeting and the training session because the ambiance may be quite different in these two types of get togethers.

Obviously, as the CEO of a growing practice, you need to prepare each day for the next day's activities. This includes mental preparation as well as physical preparation in terms of supplies and equipment. You may want to take a quiet moment in the evening and review your next day's activities, including a patient list, if possible. This helps to prepare you for whatever may come tomorrow and reinforces your continual movement in the direction of ultimate practice success. Focus is everything!

Chapter 8 Daily Critical Action Steps

A "prepractice briefing" is a meeting of your staff before your practice day begins in which you should review the day's activities. It should be an upbeat affair, not a problem-solving meeting. This is your pregame huddle, and you should end it with a "high-fives" moment. Nothing gets you more into the game plan than a prepractice briefing, which need only last 5 to 10 minutes.

An example of a daily critical action checklist is shown in **Table 8–1**.

Obviously, your chart may look quite different, but it should look something like the example. Boxes marked with an "✘" are either completed or not applicable. Your job is to complete all the other boxes each week. Always leave a few blank lines because the unexpected may occur. You may also wish to keep track of your practice statistics on the chart. Ideally, you should have a copy of this daily chart with you at all times; it serves as your compass to keep on track.

> Each man should frame life so that at some future hour, fact and his dreamings meet.
>
> —Victor Hugo

Table 8–1 *Daily Critical Action Checklist*

Week of: _____

Scheduled programs and projects: _____

Special dates and events: _____

Important notes: _____

_____

Daily Function	Mon	Tue	Wed	Thu	Fri	Sat	Sun
Inspirational reading							
Exercise							
Read vision, mission, and goals							
Prepractice briefing						✗	✗
Office-opening checklist						✗	✗
Patient notes and charts completed						✗	✗
Insurance reports completed						✗	✗
Referral letters completed						✗	✗
Accounts payable up-to-date						✗	✗
Accounts receivable billing up-to-date						✗	✗
Clinical education review						✗	✗
Weekly staff meeting	✗	✗		✗	✗	✗	✗
Scheduled programs and projects							
Prepare for next day							

Chapter 9

Final Preparations

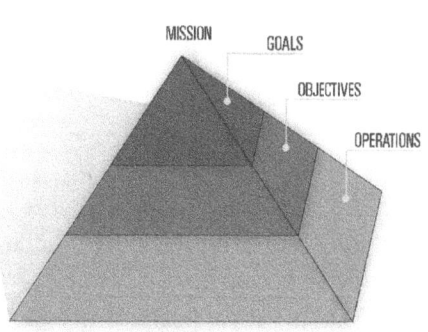

Take a breather and see what you have produced so far:

- A detailed strategic plan comprised of a vision, mission, goals, objectives, and operational tasks
- A prioritized list of action steps within a specified period of time
- A manual of rules, procedures, and policies
- A daily critical action list

> Thoroughness characterizes all successful men. Genius is the art of taking infinite pains.... All great achievement has been characterized by extreme care, infinite painstaking, even to the minutest detail.
>
> —Elbert Hubbard

(For your reference, an Executive Summary of all necessary steps in the planning process is provided in Appendix 4.)

You are just about ready to launch, and more than likely, you already have, by creating procedures and policies, forms, letters, and other documents by now. Before the formal launch, however, let me give you a basic checklist of items that ideally should be in your plan. I say "ideally" rather than "absolutely" because it is only my opinion that they should be there. Somewhere in the world, there is probably a successful and fulfilling chiropractic practice that does not incorporate my ideal list of items. Realistically, though, you should give serious consideration to including this list of minimum practice requirements somewhere in your plan.

Suggested Minimum Components of Your Strategic Plan

1. **New patient procedures**
   Every step from the first patient phone call to the consultation, examination, report of findings, and the beginning of care should be planned.

2. **Regular visit procedures**
   You should identify the individual components of a regular office visit (in my practice, I had 10 components to each office visit), as well as re-examination procedures and the handling of new complaints.

3. **Recall and reactivation procedures**
   One chiropractic sage stated that in real estate, the three most important things are location, location, location, and in chiropractic they are recall, recall, recall. Handling a large patient population means knowing when and how to contact people who have apparently dropped out, as well as contacting patients who have not been seen for a long time. Patients expect to be contacted by their chiropractor, to be counseled on good health habits, and to be challenged if they exhibit poor patterns of looking after themselves and their families. This is a very important part of any practice.

4. **Promotion**
   Promotional activities should be built right into your procedures. No practice survives long without new patients, which are your first and foremost requirement in practice. Promotional activities need to be carefully planned and executed on a continual basis. Do not count on the beneficence of the universe to simply drop new patients at your front door.

5. **Fees**
   Without new patients, a practice cannot survive for very long, and without the fees that patient care provides, it cannot survive at all. You must be able to look at your practice from a business perspective and analyze it accurately and honestly so that you are able to maximize your revenue and minimize your expenses. Planning for responsible fiscal management of your practice is essential.

Many, many more crucial activities could be included in your practice, but these five are, in my opinion, minimum requirements for any successful practice. I'd like to elaborate on each of them, giving you some suggestions for items to include in your strategic plan. Keep in mind that these truly are only suggestions. Furthermore, the reason I am giving you these suggestions at this late point in the book is to make sure that you have had the opportunity to discover for yourself the primary actions necessary for a successful practice. The exercises you have completed have produced a complete document, at least based on a first-run planning process. With your plan in hand, you can look over my suggested inclusions to identify any crucial activities that you may have overlooked.

> Can you think of anything more permanently elating than to know that you are on the right road at last?
>
> —Vernon Howard

New Patient Procedures

Your new patient procedure begins with the way the initial telephone call is handled. Make sure you include proper telephone technique (and proper office communication techniques in general) in your plan. Next, depending on your chiropractic technique or approach, you will need to specify exactly what information you want included on your consultation and examination forms. You should also describe the process of moving a patient from reception to consultation to examination—not just the physical move, but instructions for handling computer entries, chart construction, filing methods, and other administrative steps.

Then, consider exactly what information you want to convey to your new patient about yourself, your practice, and chiropractic. If this information is to be delivered in a patient lecture (or spinal health class) then this, too, must be specified and planned. Finally, the report of findings must be planned as to its format, it contents, and its administrative component.

Regular Visit Procedures

One way to systematize your regular office visit procedures is to look at each visit as an act in a giant play. In the theater, each step is planned, and each word is scripted so the director knows exactly what to expect during the performance. Obviously, that analogy is only partly relevant to the chiropractic office visit, and you must always be prepared for the unexpected. Nonetheless, you can plan the basic structure of an office visit, and this creates stability and strength in your overall office administration. Two initial tasks you should complete are to plan your record-keeping methods and design or obtain a patient chart or travel-card format. I strongly encourage you to design your own rather than purchase a ready-made form for the obvious reason of ensuring that it is customized to your strategic plan. Creating a form and having it printed is not difficult.

Here is a suggested format from my practice:

Before entering room:
1. Prepare yourself by reviewing the chart, noting the patient's progress, health status, appointment schedule.
2. Get "on purpose" (Focus only on your mission: the patient and your clinical goals for that patient.)

Enter room:
1. Begin with a bonding greeting (spirit to spirit, eye to eye, gentle touch).
2. Conduct examination with progress report (at a minimum, a brief "touch and tell").
3. Explain the need for each adjustment. (Neither minimize nor exaggerate the need for care.)
4. Give specific, gentle adjustment as necessary.
5. Pronounce each adjustment. (Example: "That was a good correction, John.")
6. As part of a patient's chiropractic education, explain some aspect of chiropractic, such as the effects of a specific level of adjustment. Some chiropractors call this "tic," or "patient regimen," and you can specify ahead of time exactly what you will cover for each visit. (It helps if you number your office visits for this procedure; for example, on visit 4, discuss the role of chiropractic in caring for children; on visit 5, discuss the need for telling others about chiropractic. This can all be preplanned in your strategic plan. In Appendix A, which is an example of a strategic plan, see item C1b6 on page 110.)
7. Make progress notes in your chart. (Somewhere in your plan, you should have an operational plan to list and explain all abbreviations used in your charts so any office staff or associates can discern your clinical notes. In most locations, this is a legal requirement.)
8. Acknowledge your patient and reinforce any specific instructions, for example, those relating to home care.
9. Indicate the exact date for the next appointment and obtain a firm commitment. (Never say, "See you in a few weeks.")
10. End with a bonding dismissal (eye-to-eye contact and a gentle touch).

You can see from this list how you can orchestrate the basic structure of each office visit and thereby create stability for yourself, your staff, and your patients. Your office visit may not proceed exactly as the example above, but at least you should give serious consideration to what an ideal office visit should look like. Also, note the various tasks arising from the above example: Create a structure for an ideal office visit; create a format for patient education, covering their first 40 visits (i.e., structured "tic"); create the necessary forms to record patient progress; train all staff on patient flow procedures; and create and post a list of abbreviations used on office charts.

Finally, you should plan your procedures and forms as necessary to handle new complaints and reexamination (which, in my opinion, should occur no less than every 12 visits).

Recall and Reactivation Procedures

Keeping track of a large patient population is an important part of any professional practice. Most chiropractors encourage their patients to maintain their health through periodic examinations and adjustments. If this is the case in your practice, then you need to establish procedures for recall and reactivation.

What do you do if, right in the middle of a treatment plan, your patient just stopped coming to the office? Ignore it? Phone and find out what happened? Obviously the latter is appropriate, but without a detailed strategic plan, a chiropractor will likely not have a stable, preplanned procedure for this situation.

Many aspects of this procedure need to be planned ahead of time: Who phones the patient? When is it appropriate to phone? What if you cannot reach the patient; how many times do you try? How do you answer the myriad of possible responses from the patient? How do you prevent such dropouts in the first place? Chiropractors who have planned these procedures have a higher compliance rate and, therefore, a busier practice with more satisfied patients.

Reactivation is the process of identifying and contacting (and, of course, making appointments for) patients who are not actively being treated, but should be seen periodically for either maintenance or follow-up care. Most patients lead very busy lives, and you, doctor, are not always their absolute top priority (sorry).

Most chiropractors have a long list of patients in this category, yet few, for reasons unknown, actually develop a formal reactivation procedure. Often it is omitted simply because it was never planned in the first place (something you will avoid with your strategic plan). Then, from time to time, it is done as an emergency procedure to correct an unexplained or seasonal slump in practice. (Does any of this sound familiar?)

Chiropractors and chiropractic assistants, like everyone else, have a great dislike and fear of being rejected. Often, reactivation procedures are not performed simply for this reason. The reasoning goes thus: Such-and-such a patient must not like me, or must not like chiropractic, otherwise they would be here. If I call them, I will be berated over the phone, so I will not do it. They end up taking the easy route—sending the patient a letter. If the patient comes back, great, if not, too bad. Sadly, this is a common way to deal with the reactivation issue.

Chiropractic consultants suggest that mailing a reactivation letter yields a 2 to 3 percent response, and a follow-up phone call yields about a 7 to 8 percent response. Even if these numbers are correct, it certainly justifies a reactivation program if you have several hundred or more inactive patients. However, my own research suggests a much higher yield from a follow-up phone call. Also, my data will show you why patients do not book reactivation appointments. When you see these reasons you will realize, once and for all, that fear should never keep you from contacting inactive patients.

Table 9-1 shows the results of 570 phone calls made to inactive patients. Initially, these patients were sent a very simple letter that, in fact, yielded very few appointments. As it turns out, there is quite a science to choosing the wording of a letter like this, and different consultants have different approaches, all claiming effectiveness. Our letter was as follows:

> Dear Patient,
>
> According to our records it has been _____ months since your last visit to our clinic.
>
> Our purpose is to assist as many people as possible to achieve optimum health. We are committed to our purpose and want you to know that we are vitally interested in your health status.
>
> At this time, it is highly recommended that you visit our office for a periodic check-up. This includes a review of your general health, your personal health goals, and a review of your posture and spinal alignment, and, a corrective spinal adjustment, if necessary.
>
> Please call 555-1234 to schedule your visit.
>
> Sincerely,
>
> Dr. Michael Wiles

Within about 2 weeks of sending this letter, I had my staff call the nonresponders with a message that went something like this:

> CA: This is (*name*) calling from _____ (*name of clinic*). The reason I am calling is to see if you received the letter we sent you recently.
>
> Former patient: Yes, I did/No, I did not.
>
> CA: Well, let me explain. Dr. Wiles has set aside some time over the next few weeks to help his former patients make sure they are as healthy as possible. He asked me to call you to set up an appointment since it has been so long since we last saw you. Can I set up an appointment?
>
> Former patient: Yes (appointment made) or no.

CA: (if patient says "no") Fine. Would you mind me asking if there is any reason why you wouldn't make an appointment at this time?

Former patient: (gives reason)

CA: Thank you for telling me, and I'd like to invite you to let us know if we can be of any help in the future. Bye.

Now, there are probably a hundred things wrong with both the letter and the follow-up phone call, I realize that. In fact, in later reactivation programs I changed a lot of this procedure. However, I am reprinting this letter and script to show you the results I obtained using them.

Take a look at **Table 9–1**, which represents the results of 570 phone calls made by my staff. Let me offer my interpretation of these data.

First, look at the results of "appointment made": 269 appointments from 570 phone calls (or 47.2 percent response)! I'm sure you will agree that it is worth sending approximately 600 letters and phoning 570 patients to get 269 appointments. Remember that these are patients who knew us and were not strangers or walk-ins.

Table 9–1 *Reactivation Program, Results of 570 Follow-up Phone Calls by Four Chiropractic Assistants*

	N	Appointment made	1*	2*	3*	4*	5*	6*	7*	Appointment average
CA 1	109	52	7	21	7	2	1	3	16	0.477
CA 2	196	107	25	38	12	2	0	3	9	0.546
CA 3	57	22	7	14	1	2	2	5	4	0.386
CA 4	208	88	24	65	7	1	2	5	16	0.423
Total	570	269	63	138	27	7	5	16	45	0.472
% response		47.2	11.1	24.2	4.7	1.2	0.9	2.8	7.9	

CA = Chiropractic assistant
N = Number of calls made by each CA
*Reasons for not making appointments:
1. No perceived health problem ("I feel fine...")
2. Priority and scheduling problem ("busy," "will call you later")
3. Financial concern ("can't afford")
4. Poor previous results ("didn't help")
5. Credibility issue or social conflict ("MD or family advised against care")
6. Other DC is closer or patient has moved ("Seeing other DC")
7. "Other" (includes moved, patient vague or unable to give reason, and other responses that do not fall under other categories)

Next look at the appointment average (like a batting average) of the four CAs who made the calls. You can see that all their averages are in a relatively small range, indicating approximately equal effectiveness on the phone. CA2, with the highest average, was the youngest and somewhat more assertive than the others. CA3 was probably the most passive or least assertive. These data suggest that a healthy level of assertiveness is helpful in telephone communications with patients. Also, the different averages reflect the different times of day when the CAs were able to call the patients.

Now, look at the reasons that patients gave when they did NOT book an appointment.

- 11.1 percent
  Patients stated that they "felt fine" and that, in their opinion, no appointment was necessary at this time. This is, as the old joke goes, good news and bad news. The good news is that they did, in fact, feel fine and had a good impression of our office in this regard. The bad news is that they needed education about chiropractic and preventive care, in which case they would have appreciated the need for periodic check-ups and adjustments.

- 24.2 percent
  Patients said they were "busy" and stated that they would call us when they felt they could get in for a check-up. Now, I had enough dates as a teenager to know a brush-off when I get one, and this is probably what a lot of these were. However, the good news is that they were all basically friendly (my CAs did not experience any patient-initiated phone disconnections at all) and more than likely had a good impression of me and our office. In fact, many did call later.

- 4.7 percent
  Patients felt that they could not (or would not) afford chiropractic care. A lot of chiropractors still have a problem with money (that is, collecting it), and sadly, this is reflected in their inability to talk to patients about money. Well, if this describes you, then these results should help. Only 27 patients out of 570 calls stated that money was an issue in continuing care!

- 1.2 percent
  Patients said they did not make an appointment because they felt that chiropractic did not help them or did not help them enough. It is noteworthy that no patients stated that they were worse from treatment. To be honest—and I did not think it has anything to do with my chiropractic skill—I think this is an incredibly low number. Can you think of any other health practitioner's sample of 570 patients that you could

phone and discover that only 1.2 percent, or 7 patients, were not helped? This is a tribute to the chiropractic profession.

- 0.9 percent
  Five patients had been advised by another practitioner or a family member not to continue with chiropractic services for a variety of reasons.

- 2.8 percent
  Patients were seeing another chiropractor (or another type of provider) for a variety of reasons, the most common of which was proximity to workplace or their home.

- 7.9 percent
  Patients gave vague or unclassifiable reasons for not making an appointment, including having moved. Some elderly patients had died.

So, here is what all of this means: Out of 570 calls placed by four CAs to inactive patients, only 39 did not make appointments because of financial reasons, lack of previous results, or medical advice. Many chiropractors fear these three responses, yet these data suggest that such fears are unwarranted. With good patient education (see the suggested operational steps in the sample plans in the appendices), more patients from categories 1 and 2 in **Table 9–1** would have made appointments, raising the appointment percentage even higher than the already-impressive 47.2 percent.

> Far better it is to dare mighty things, to win glorious triumphs, even though checkered by failure, than to rank with those poor spirits who neither enjoy much nor suffer much, because they live in the grey twilight that knows neither victory nor defeat.
>
> — Theodore Roosevelt

Bottom line: Make sure you have a well-planned and well-executed recall and reactivation program.

Promotion

Dr. C. J. Mertz has been quoted as saying, "Your procedures are your promotions and your promotions are your procedures." I certainly agree with this concept. As you review your strategic plan, make sure that there is a promotional aspect to as much of it as possible. Think about what this means. Everyone should have a family chiropractor, but only a small percentage of people actually do. Until everyone does, we all have to take some responsibility for promoting chiropractic and natural health principles. Therefore, since we are the agents of chiropractic, we should be promoting ourselves. How you do this is your responsibility, but make sure that you do it. New patients are the lifeblood of chiropractic, and you don't want an anemic practice.

As you assemble and create your strategic plan, many operational items naturally fall in the area of practice promotion, education, or marketing. You may want to separate those items into another document called your annual marketing calendar. You will see this operational step in the sample plan in Appendix 1 (objective D3). Constructing an annual marketing calendar gives you an overview of all promotional events that are planned for one year. By studying the results of your promotional activities, you can literally predict the number of new patients you will be seeing over the next year.

There are many ways to create a marketing calendar but the simplest is to plan promotional events on a weekly schedule (such as spinal health classes, sometimes called special consultations), a monthly schedule (such as outside speaking engagements), a quarterly schedule (such as newsletters and open houses), and a yearly schedule (such as seasonal events around national holidays and special days such as Mother's Day). Then, write every promotional event on your calendar; a large wall-mounted calendar that the entire staff can see is ideal. You will be amazed that you now have many, many items planned over the next year.

Obviously this calendar of events has to be derived from your prioritized lists of operational tasks from your strategic plan, but you can see how these events accumulate until your calendar is full and you are constantly promoting yourself and chiropractic. As I said, how you do this is up to you. Some doctors enjoy public screenings, others enjoy public speaking, and others enjoy writing for local newspapers. That is the joy of the strategic planning process; you get to choose the promotional events that you enjoy.

Here is one more thing about promotions that may help you organize your plan and your events. You can categorize promotions to keep organized and to help you balance your promotions over a number of different methods. Among the many ways to do this are two that I would like to recommend.

The first approach is to categorize promotions by their method of delivery. There are four basic ways to promote:

- Through literature, mail, and written media
- Through speaking engagements and public appearances
- Through joint efforts and alliances with stores, other professionals, and other organizations
- Through specialized programs (such as a runner's clinic)

Another way to categorize your promotional activities is by the nature of the promotion and its target audience. Promotions can be either internal (directed at your current patients) or external (directed at nonpatients). They can also be procedural events built into your regular practice activities as standing plans (such as spinal care classes or the production and mailing of a newsletter), or they can be special events that occur irregularly as single-use plans (such as a practice opening event or an internal promotion coinciding with a community event like a charity run). Therefore, you are able to categorize your promotions as follows:

- Type I: internal and procedural
- Type II: internal and special
- Type III: external and procedural
- Type IV: external and special

These simple ways of looking at your promotions will help you make sure that your promotions are balanced or at least spread out among various methods.

Fees

I have avoided talking about the financial aspects of practice up to this point. However, you need to eat and survive, and you have to deal with a definite bottom line to stay in practice. You cannot help others if you are struggling yourself, so you should not deny that making a comfortable living can be a wonderful extrinsic benefit of being a chiropractor. Money cannot buy happiness, but it can provide you with peace of mind so that you can benefit society as a healer. "I was born with nothing and I still have most of it," should not be your vision statement.

> The doctor who charges nothing is worth nothing.
> —Maimonedes

In this section, I give you some tips to help you make sure that your strategic plan covers relevant financial considerations. First, here are the seven most common mistakes that chiropractors make regarding the handling of fees in the office and the communication of fee-related issues:

- Discussing fees midway through the examination
  Obviously this is a major error in procedure, but unfortunately it is a common occurrence. Avoid this error by ensuring that fees are discussed as an office procedure before any professional services are rendered.

- Apologizing for fees
  If a fair, appropriate, and professional fee policy is established as part of your strategic plan, then you can be proud of it and stand by it. Never apologize for the privilege of earning a living as a chiropractor. This error is common among new graduates, probably because of insecurity.

- Asking about a patient's financial situation
  To put it bluntly, your patient's financial situation is none of your business. Despite this, chiropractors often feel drawn into the financial

despair of patients. If you want to have a special fee structure for charity cases, then plan it (see the sample plan in Appendix 1, item B1b2) and use it when appropriate.

- Being vague or evasive about fees
  By now, you must be getting the big picture of strategic planning, and you can see how this type of mistake would never happen with a properly planned practice. If you have a formal fee structure and a formal new patient procedure, then simply follow procedure and you never have to worry about being evasive or vague when discussing fees. The only other concern you might have is staff members who do not follow standard operating procedures. In this case, they require either training or dismissal.

- Discussing fees with the wrong person
  This is actually a common concern among chiropractors and other health professionals. You can avoid this by establishing an appropriate new patient procedure in which you identify the person responsible for the fees.

- Making assumptions
  You know the scenario. You think Mr. Jones is destitute and give him a reduced fee. Then you watch him drive home in his brand-new Mercedes-Benz. Proper planning and adherence to office procedure helps avoid such situations.

- Getting involved in details
  To avoid this mistake, simply have a standard office procedure for handling the small details of fees, such as method of payment, and the calculations of exact amounts, giving most or all of these duties to your CA.

> Go out and buy yourself a five-cent pencil and a ten-cent notebook and begin to write down some million-dollar ideas for yourself.
>
> —Bob Grinde

We have all made some of these mistakes in the past. Just make sure that your strategic plan has appropriate procedures or policies to handle all these concerns, and you will never make these mistakes again.

A common concern in chiropractic practice is knowing when to offer a low or competitive fee. Here are three suggested situations calling for either a low fee or a fee lower than or equal to your competitors:

- New patient consultation and examination
  In most chiropractic practices, the highest single-fee item is the new-patient examination. Unfortunately, for prospective new patients, this can be a decisive factor for not choosing chiropractic care. Reducing

this fee is a wise decision, because your highest overall fees are derived from patient care, not from examination.

- Emergencies
  In emergency situations, it is a good idea to be convenient not only in terms of time, but also in terms of fees. People are desperate in emergencies and do not appreciate being taken advantage of when it comes to fees. (We all know the helpless and annoying frustration of paying exorbitant fees in a home emergency, such as a plumbing or electrical failure.) By being fair in an emergency situation, you will gain lasting respect and appreciation from your patients.

- Urgencies
  These are office visits of an urgent, unexpected nature, such as a sudden recurrence of an old problem. Treat them as you would emergencies and do not charge an excessive fee at a time when the patient has no other choice. Certainly, do not give away your services; charge a fair fee. But do not take advantage of your patients' misfortune by overcharging.

The above three suggestions could be incorporated into your strategic plan in terms of new patient and regular patient procedures.

Finally, have a firm financial policy regarding accounts payable, and make sure that it is clear and communicated to each patient. Your financial policy should include methods of payment and your method of handling overdue accounts, including rate of interest charged, among other things.

> I've been rich and I've been poor. Rich is better.
>
> —attributed to Mae West

The Five Ps of Professional Success

Many years ago, I read an article in the *American Medical News* (a publication of the American Medical Association) called "the three As to professional success." The three As were ability, availability, and affability.

This article stated that the general public felt that all doctors generally had the same abilities. In other words, most patients never inquire about their doctor's medical school marks and simply assume that doctors all do the same type of work. The variables, then, in determining your success are more likely to be availability and affability. The article went on to say that you had to be available (make your office hours convenient for most patients) and affable, or likable.

Simple as this advice may be, I think it is very valuable. Time after time, I talk to struggling chiropractors and discover that they have a strange schedule of office hours. You know what I mean: Monday from 9 to 12; Tuesday from 8 to 10, and then from 1 to 4; Wednesday off; Thursday from 9 to 1 and 2 to 6; and so on. Here's a real simple suggestion: Offer regular hours every day (maybe the best thing the AMA has done for you in years).

Finally, being affable should not be a difficult thing for a chiropractor. But if you feel you need work in this area, then kudos to you for your honesty. Go find a mentor, read personal development literature, or, if necessary, get professional help. After all you have been through to become a chiropractor, don't let your attitude ruin your career.

I would like to offer my own formula for professional success and go two better than the AMA. Here are the five Ps of professional success:

1. Personality

    I agree with the AMA that affability is a key factor in professional success. I think we can go beyond this trait, however, and look at a broad range of personality characteristics that promote a successful career. This includes many positive qualities such as empathy, understanding, cheerfulness, industry, assertiveness, compassion, kindness, and many others. Here is the key: Never stop working on yourself; keep searching for ways to improve your relationships and personal growth.

2. Philosophy

    A big concern I have about our profession is the apparent lack of a unified philosophy underlying our approach to patient care and our professional lives. This book is not a forum for discussing philosophy, but I would simply offer this advice: Whatever your personal philosophy about chiropractic, the healing process, and your role in the world, articulate it, at least for yourself. Force yourself to identify what you actually believe. This may not be easy for some of you, but it is a necessary task to give you passion for your work. I hope this passion became evident to you in the earliest exercises in this book when you created a vision statement. If the whole exercise of planning has itself been a journey of discovery, then you may wish to go back and revisit the first exercises.

3. Planning
   I cannot emphasize enough the need for proper planning as a requirement for any successful enterprise. In fact, I wrote a whole book about it! (Need I say more?)

4. Procedure
   Obviously this follows the above item. As a strategic planner, you now know how procedure emanates from your vision, mission, goals, and objectives. Ultimately, your procedures are what gives stability to your practice as well as what defines your practice as the unique practice it is. Make sure that you do not get tempted to incorporate someone else's procedures into your practice just because they sound good or may have worked for someone else. This is not to say that you cannot use or incorporate such procedures, but just make sure that they fit into a need in your own personal plan. Always plan from *above-down* and do not change your goals or objectives just to fit a procedure that sounds good. If it fits, use it.

5. Persistence
   This final P is possibly the most important one. Without a persistent and passionate approach to building your practice, you may not succeed at all. You can be guaranteed that setbacks and challenges will find you, especially when you least expect them. No other words or advice can help you at those times except to persist, persist, and persist. You simply must be tough enough inside to handle what happens on the outside.

> Firmness of purpose is one of the best instruments of success.
>
> —Lord Chesterfield

Chapter 10

On Your Mark, Get Set…

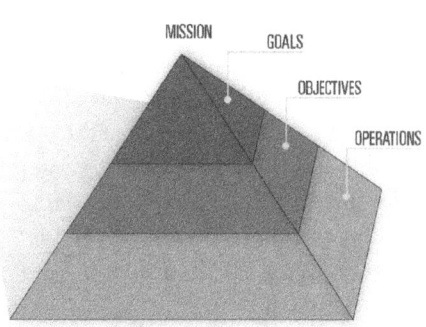

You have already taken that single step.

Your journey can take you to your vision, and this is a very powerful thing indeed. You started this strategic planning process with the development of a vision statement. Now, at the end of the planning process, complete the circle by returning to this starting place of your journey.

> A journey of a thousand miles begins with a single step.
> —Lao Tzu

The vision statement you created in exercise 3 has to be an ongoing driving force for you from now on. It has to be something that you awaken with and something that follows you like a loyal pet all through the day. It must become part of your soul and in the background of your every thought and action.

The word *vision* has many definitions, including "a thing or idea perceived vividly in the imagination." Your task is to give life to this thing that you have called your vision. Through the completion of 18 exercises, you have developed a complete strategy to bring your vision to life. Although I have stressed the importance of action in completing this plan, there is one other critical step we have not really talked about—*visualization*.

To visualize is defined as "to make visible." This is exactly what you want—to create, or make visible, something that is perceived vividly in your imagination.

One of the most commonly used techniques employed daily by ultrasuccessful people is visualization. With this incredibly powerful process, you first assume a quiet, comfortable, and relaxed position, and then you vividly imagine in your mind *exactly* that which you wish to make real. The science and art of visualization is beyond the scope of this planning manual, and you are encouraged to seek further information on this topic if you are new to it. For now, let me assure you that there is great power in the ability to visualize your practice in as much detail as possible.

Close your eyes and see the reception room exactly as you have planned it. See the patients happily waiting and ready to see you. See the staff smiling at you as you enter the office. Try to be as detailed as possible with your visualization process. See colors, smell and feel the furniture and surroundings. W. Clement Stone once said that what the mind could vividly perceive, it could achieve.

Everything begins with a vision. Your planning adventure began with the creation of a vision statement. Elaborate on that statement in your mind on a daily basis until it literally becomes a reality before your very eyes. Your carefully designed action steps will easily accomplish what your eyes have repeatedly seen, and your subconscious mind will look for serendipitous ways to continually move you toward the successful completion of your plan.

> Until one is committed, there is hesitancy, the chance to draw back, always ineffectiveness. Concerning all acts of initiative (and creation), there is one elementary truth the ignorance of which kills countless ideas and splendid plans: that the moment one definitely commits oneself, then Providence moves too. All sorts of things occur to help one that would never otherwise have occurred. A whole stream of events issues from the decision, raising in one's favor all manner of unforeseen incidents and meetings and material assistance which no man could have dreamed would come his way. Whatever you can do or dream you can do, begin it. Boldness has genius, power and magic in it. Begin it now.
>
> —*Goethe*

Appendix 1

Strategic Plan Example A

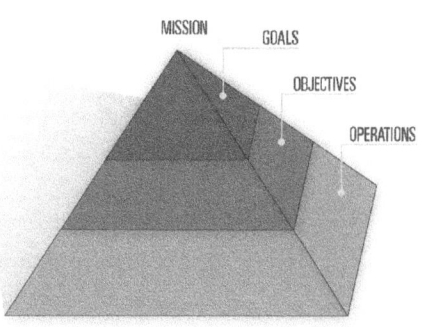

This plan is an example of the structure of the strategic plan for a solo doctor with a traditional chiropractic family practice and an emphasis on clinical excellence and marketing. Note the naming and numbering system as described in the text. Objectives without an operational task (for example, A5) become the operational task. This strategic plan is typical with 4 goals, 16 objectives, and 129 operational tasks.

Vision
We have the most unique chiropractic family practice in the world.

Mission
To operate a unique chiropractic clinic that has a worldwide reputation for excellence in health-care delivery. The quality, effectiveness, and distinctiveness of our services are characterized by the delivery of a complete program of care that includes symptomatic, corrective, and maintenance phases, as well as patient education about chiropractic and the healing process. Our aim is to provide our services to as many people as possible.

Goals

A. *Office management and physical plant*
   To successfully manage our human resources and physical plant to support our mission
   (Statistic: total visits)

B. ***Fees and accounts***
   To control costs and maximize revenue to provide resources for the survival and growth of the practice and staff
   (Statistic: fees charges and collected)

C. ***Quality care delivery***
   To deliver the highest quality of chiropractic care to all patients
   (Statistic: office visit average; goal: 40 or more)

D. ***Marketing—general***
   To identify and develop specific action plans to attract as many new patients as possible to our practice
   (Statistic: total NPs)

   Objective D4: Internal marketing program
   To develop a specific marketing approach, including patient education programs to attract new patient referrals from our existing patients
   (Statistic: referred NPs)

   Objective D5: External marketing program
   To effectively promote our services to the general public to provide a constant supply of new patients
   (Statistic: nonreferred NPs)

Objectives and Operational Tasks

A1 To determine maximum efficient patient capacity and have an appropriate scheduling software program

A2 To use effective communication techniques in all office communications

   A2a Use effective telephone techniques, including appropriate scripts.

   A2b Use effective closing techniques.

   A2c Use effective standards for appearance and presentation of office, doctors, and staff, including dress codes, office atmosphere, and music.

   A2d Develop a logo for use on all stationary, forms, uniforms, and other practice materials.

   A2e Develop a complete set of up-to-date, first-class forms for patient and office use.

A2f Develop appropriate scripts for doctor to use in specific circumstances.

A3 To use effective and efficient appointment scheduling procedures

    A3a Refine and develop effective new patient procedures, including a formal NP brochure (NP kit).

    A3b Use multiple appointment program (MAP) whenever possible.

    A3c Instill in patients the need to keep their appointments and follow through with recommended care. (CAs should constantly talk about positive results. All patients should be offered a choice of two appointments. Maintain control; no patient should leave the office without an appointment.)

    A3d Call patients to remind them of appointments whenever more than 3 weeks have elapsed between visits.

    A3e Call all missed appointments within 15 minutes to reschedule, and keep log of all missed appointments and results of efforts to reschedule.

    A3f Keep statistics of patients who come in for scheduled appointments each week; measure both as numbers and percentage. (For example, on Friday you have 300 visits booked for the next week. By next Friday, you have seen 310 during the week, but only 240, or 80 percent of the original 300, kept their appointments.)

A4 To have an effective physical plant to support our mission

    A4a Ensure that office is visible via appropriate signs.

        A4b1 Ensure a noteworthy and educational reception room through decoration and accessories. (Ideas: office mascot, updated doctor's CV)

        A4b2 Ensure a fully functional and clean reception desk and work area.

    A4c Establish a properly furnished and equipped patient education center for reports of finding.

    A4d Establish specific room functions and names (for example, examination room, adjustment room, therapy room, and patient education center) and use the office tour as part of every NP's orientation.

- A4e Establish a routine method of physical plant review, and identify the actual needs of the physical plant as well as a maintenance schedule and standards (that is, use a monthly checklist). (For example, standards could include no dirty gowns ever left in room, no equipment on floor, diagnostic equipment spotlessly clean, and adjusting table upholstery intact.)

A5 To define all office policies in a current manual, including financial policy, appointment policy, employment policy, roles for specific CAs, staff meetings, and other policies as required

B1 To maintain an efficient and effective fee schedule and collection system designed to minimize accounts receivable

- B1a Establish a fee schedule for all services rendered and a catalog of services and products sold.
- B1b Establish, as part of an overall fee schedule, special fees for unique groups.
    - B1b1 Company chiropractor program
    - B1b2 Charity cases; establish criteria and fixed fees
    - B1b3 Family fees
- B1c Establish firm front-desk procedure and control methods.
    - B1c1 Develop financial consultation by CA at report of findings.
    - B1c2 Develop and use a letter and follow-up phone call for practice dropouts based on financial concerns, with offer to reduce fees if they resume care within 15 days. (Research shows dental experience: 134 cards mailed, 26 reactivations within 15 days.)
- B1d Establish firm policy for overdue accounts (0–30 days: grace; 31–60 days: past due; 61–90 days: red stamp and phone call; more than 90 days: collection agency).

B2 To develop specialized fee arrangements and tracking systems for workers' compensation and personal injury patients

- B2a Establish method of tracking workers' compensation accounts and ensure appropriate billing procedures.
- B2b Establish method of tracking personal injury accounts and ensure appropriate and timely billing procedures.

B2c Establish an insurance file containing names of friendly and cooperating companies and agents, those that approve direct billing, for example.

  B2c1 Nurture those contacts with regular mailings of reprints and information.

B3 **Keep fee schedule current and review fees to effectively charge for all services rendered**

  B3a Perform annual fee review of local competitors.

  B3b Establish annual review of all fees, services, and policies.

  B3c Establish annual review of office expenses to maximize effectiveness and minimize overhead.

B4 **To engage the services of a competent accountant to perform an annual financial review and statement of income and expenses**

  B4a In consultation with the accountant, determine the most appropriate method of accounting for office receivables and payables.

C1 **To develop and offer high-quality patient care programs (to remove quality interference to practice growth)**

  C1a Develop new patient programs.

   C1a1 Develop a formal NP kit (see A3a).

   C1a2 Develop and use a thorough and personalized consultation and examination format for NPs.

   C1a3 For report of findings (ROF), develop a report of findings package that includes a doctor's manual of sequenced diagrams in a binder and a written report for patients covering the total health package (pain relief, restoral of health, maintenance/elective care); also include a letter sent to all NPs after their report of findings.

    C1a3a Develop a formal report after reassessments similar to the ones used for C1a3.

    C1a3b Develop a formal initial patient education program (primary objectives over the first four visits: subluxation, adjustment, families, health restoration, and lifetime health maintenance).

C1a3c Develop a special procedure for patients who do not accept recommendations at the ROF (day 1: report; day 10, if patient does not return: letter sent indicating benefits of services and including names of satisfied patients, with their permission; day 15, if still no show: phone call, always scripted, with message exactly same as in letter and asking if they have any reason why they should not proceed. Research indicates acceptance by one-third of patients using this method.

C1a4 Always promptly acknowledge and thank referral sources.

C1b Develop regular patient programs.

C1b1 Be familiar with as many treatment systems as possible and specialize in various aspects of some of these.

C1b2 Define and develop specialty interest areas (e.g., pediatrics, posture, sports injuries, female problems, geriatrics, and personal injury cases).

C1b3 Be familiar with modern chiropractic methods of acute and chronic pain control (including electrotherapy and laser).

C1b4 Be knowledgeable about all major exercise programs related to major pain syndromes.

C1b5 Regularly keep up with all paperwork such as insurance reports and referral letters.

C1b6 Keep patients enthusiastic about their care, throughout their care program, by using the techniques of PTC (present time consciousness), ICA (I care attitude), and *tic*.

C1b7 Be aware of, support, and contribute to the research and clinical literature, including the development of an office research agenda.

C1b8 Develop and use regular reexamination protocols and systems that provide for objective measurement of improvement.

C1b8a Develop and use specific protocol and forms for initial consultation and examination and for reexamination of patients in specific categories such as whiplash protocol, orthotics, headache, LBP, general health, pediatrics, TMJ, carpal tunnel syndrome, and postural correction.

C1b8b Develop mechanisms for short-term and long-term follow-up of patients who do not wish maintenance/elective care.

C1b9 Develop firm protocol, including scripts, for managing missed appointments (that is, phone calls, follow-up letter, and other strategies).

Strategic Plan Example A

C2   To develop and use an effective system of health review, promotion, and maintenance (remove quantity interference to practice growth)

    C2a   Develop maintenance/elective care programs.

        C2a1   Develop a special procedure for initiation of maintenance care (for example, special letter congratulating patient, specialized health promotion material, VIP mailings, and discounts on purchases of supplies). (An example of a letter to a patient who is beginning maintenance care is shown on page 117.)

        C2a2   Provide a method of regular health assessment on a monthly basis (for example, Project HOPE, Health Opportunity by Periodic Evaluation, originally described by Dr. James Parker).

            C2a2a   Establish an annual health calendar for Project HOPE (for example, January: BP; February: urinalysis; March: height and weight; April: flexibility).

    C2b   Develop family health promotion and review.

        C2b1   Develop and use forms and protocols for regular collection of family health data.

            C2b1a   Family registration form for all NPs

            C2b1b   Semiannual family health questionnaire (stresses need for doctor to know all family health problems)

        C2b2   Use mechanism and procedure for screening all children of patients for scoliosis, postural distortion, and subluxations.

    C2c   Develop reactivation and recall procedures.

        C2c1   Develop and use a routine method of recall and reactivation of inactive patients.

            C2c1a   Recall (short term) principles:

                1. Specificity (to make sure ____ does not happen, not just to check things out)

                2. Repetition (tell them over and over and precondition them when patients first come in)

                3. Personal (no left messages; personal contact only)

            C2c1b   Reactivation (long term) principles:

                1. Letter initially (2% to 3% response)

                2. Follow-up phone call (7% to 8% response or higher, see page 93); always use scripts and emphasize the consequences of no care (e.g., why they should come in)

Appendix 1 Strategic Plan Example A

D1 To promote our practice ethically to as many groups as possible, including specific plans for each of the following groups:

  D1a Internal
  1. Regular patients (VIPs)
  2. Regular patients (all others)

  D1b External
  1. Local residents (nonpatients)
  2. MDs and DOs
  3. Local DCs
  4. Local industries
  5. DPMs
  6. DDSs (regarding TMJ)
  7. ODs (regarding neck pain, headaches, and posture)
  8. Health clubs
  9. Civic groups and organizations
  10. Schools

  D1c Special case
  Develop methods that will attract children into our practice, such as Kids Klinics.

D2 To determine an annual marketing budget as part of overall financial planning

D3 To develop an annual marketing calendar to provide advance notice of events for proper planning (for example, Mother's Day) and that incorporates all marketing activities listed in strategic plan

D4 To develop a specific marketing approach, including patient education programs, to attract new patient referrals from our existing patients (Statistic: referred new patients)

  D4a Develop a specific internal marketing program.

   D4a1 Establish an effective staff training program to create a front desk climate of passion and enthusiasm for chiropractic (may include staff business cards, staff referral contests, and other strategies).

   D4a2 Develop a strategy for repositioning patients from short-term relief to long-term family care.

   D4a3 Develop and use internal market research methods to determine what patients want (for example, feedback from patient surveys).

D4b Develop a referral management program.

  D4b1 Conduct referral source analysis and develop plan to increase referrals.

  D4b2 Continually review our services looking for special areas that will promote referrals (for example, broad range of services and differentiation from others).

  D4b3 Elements of referral management program

    D4b3a Ask for referrals. Develop scripts and practice them. Develop patient recruiting package, special procedures and offers for family members, and ask patients about clubs or groups that we could speak to, and other ideas.

    D4b3b Have up-to-date curriculum vitae in reception room. (To increase word-of-mouth referrals, you must establish the image of an expert; ask for referrals and reinforce behavior with recognition from doctor.)

    D4b3c Have practice brochure and NP kit.

    D4b3d Engage in internal prospecting activities (for example, make visit to office the highlight of patients' day; send out mailings; contact each patient household at least four times per year).

    D4b3e Frequent referrer program

      1. Reinforce referring behavior.

        a. Phone ("Thank you. We'll take good care of your friend, we consider you a special friend of our practice.")

        b. Handwritten note and gift (inexpensive gifts such as inscribed spine key rings)

      2. Reward multiple referrals (series of gifts for second, third, fourth referrals with significant gifts for fifth referral and higher).

      3. Send all gifts with a powerful letter.

      4. Hold regular patient appreciation days and events.

        a. Open to all patients; minimum of one a year

        b. Special invitation to referral sources; two or three times a year, with at least one big event for multiple referrers (for example, group goes to major league baseball game)

Appendix 1 Strategic Plan Example A

        D4b3f Develop specific methods for recording all referral sources and immediately and effectively acknowledging referrals.

            1. From patients (see D4b3e)
            2. From MDs (letter, referral pad, information sheet about us)
            3. From occupational nurses (letter, referral pads, information sheets)
            4. From others (include information sheet about our office)

D4c Develop a patient education program.

     D4c1 Develop and implement a patient education program integrated with the care program, including motivational material to keep patients enthusiastic and interested in their care.

     D4c2 Develop and use specific, selected literature and videos in patient care that encourage and promote referral consciousness.

          D4c2a Prepare patient information sheets on home care for each major pain syndrome.

          D4c2b Prepare patient information sheets on menopause, cholesterol, osteoporosis, and other hot topics.

          D4c2c Ensure that correct and useful information is available in each part of the office (every room should have something).

          D4c2d Have effective video education wherever possible.

     D4c3 Develop regular informational mailings to patients and referral sources.

          D4c3a Regular quarterly newsletter; always have a limited-time call to action

              D4c3a1   VIP mailing more frequently

          D4c3b Industrial care newsletter to local industry

          D4c3c Legal newsletter to local attorneys

          D4c3d Medical newsletter to local nurses and physicians

          D4c3e Other informational bulletins (always include limited-time call to action)

     D4c4 Develop and implement a formal back school program.

D4d Develop a spinal care class.

     D4d1 Develop and use a specific protocol for getting patients to commit to attend a biweekly spinal health class.

        D4d2   Develop and use a specific spinal care class that contains information about our clinic and chiropractic and concludes with a promotional offer.

  D4e   Develop other internal promotions.

        D4e1   Use unusual promotion dates to generate enthusiasm.

                D4e1a   Ethnic holidays

                D4e1b   Office anniversaries (try to have something each month)

        D4e2   Use various seasonal, thematic, or ongoing promotions to generate enthusiasm from patients.

                D4e2a   Clinic diet program

                D4e2b   Back school throughout the year

                D4e2c   Posture screening program (ongoing)

        D4e3   Use specific family- and children-oriented promotions to build a family practice.

                D4e3a   Family: family plans, family of the month

                D4e3b   Children: chirokid club, photos, educational center, Kids Klinic

D5   To effectively promote our services to the general public to provide a constant supply of new patients (Statistic: nonreferred NPs)

  D5a   Develop an effective long-range external marketing program.

        D5a1   Use a community advisory panel of local people to meet with us and discuss our role in the community (four to six people, quarterly basis).

        D5a2   Use external marketing research methods to determine what our public wants and demands.

        D5a3   Develop formal public relations program, including press contacts and methodology for press releases.

  D5b   Promote our services through literature, mail, and written media.

        D5b1   Write articles for local papers on newsworthy topics (for example, posture in high school students)

        D5b2   Seek opportunity to write column each week for one or more newspapers.

        D5b3   Identify local ethnic groups and produce material in their language (especially first-class brochures).

        D5b4   Develop system and protocol of mailing neighborhood flyers as part of overall marketing program.

	D5b5	Consider "Val-Pack" concept for local residents.
	D5b6	Assemble nonpatient mailing list for sending patients' newsletter; assemble list by collecting business cards (exchange business cards throughout community, every day).
D5c		Promote our services through joint efforts with others.
	D5c1	Develop joint promotion efforts with local noncompeting professionals (identify them, brainstorm, proposal, promotion).
	D5c2	Publish and promote a free eight-page quarterly newspaper called Community Health News by selling space to local professionals. (Selling space covers cost of publication and distribution. You are editor, so you have front-page coverage and control what goes in the paper.)
D5d		Promote our services through speaking engagements and public appearances.
	D5d1	Sponsor free public lectures on various topics of interest (for example, longevity, wellness, stress, and LBP). Ideal frequency is one per week; prepare the schedule for 3 months at a time (distribute list to schools, clubs, libraries, health centers, and other community groups).
	D5d2	Develop a public-speaking agenda (major topics only) with targeted audiences. (Plan six speeches per year for 3 years.)
	D5d3	Develop a health and wellness speaker's group with other professionals in the community.
	D5d4	Develop and sponsor public seminars on major public interest topics (for example, how to relax).
	D5d5	Approach libraries, community colleges, and schools to offer night-school programs on various popular topics (for example, how to look after your spine).
D5e		Promote our services through specialized programs.
	D5e1	Develop a foot care program, including orthotic prescription and dispensing.
	D5e2	Develop a thorough industrial care strategy, including all industry (systematically). Offer back school, company doctor, newsletter, pre-employment screening, and ergonomic report programs.
	D5e3	Develop repetitive strain program.
	D5e4	Offer specific sports-oriented services (for example, a runner's clinic and fitness analysis).
	D5e5	Develop fibromyalgia and chronic fatigue syndrome programs.
D5f		Promote our services through miscellaneous promotions.

Here is a copy of the maintenance letter mentioned in item C2a1.

Dear Patient and Friend:

CONGRATULATIONS! You have now completed a program of corrective chiropractic care and are now beginning a program of preventive maintenance for your spine and nervous system.

What seemed like a long road when you first began your corrective care program is now over, and you can look forward to a state of improved well-being as a result.

Now, it is very important for you to incorporate a number of health safeguards to maintain what you have achieved. Six crucial steps are as follows:

1. Observe rules of proper lifting; most important, do not bend and twist at the same time.
2. Avoid unnecessary stress; do not overwork or overplay.
3. Eat a well-balanced diet of nutritious foods.
4. Keep in good overall physical condition with moderate exercise.
5. Get adequate rest, and use a proper pillow and mattress.
6. Have regular spinal examinations for proper nerve function.

Pay special attention to these steps, and you will maximize your health potential and quality of life. Finally, if any new health problems occur, please let us know immediately, so we can provide the earliest possible care. In particular, look out for the following warning signs of stress affecting the nervous system: restless sleep; fatigue; headache; neck, shoulder, or back pain; irritability or nervousness. Should any of these develop between maintenance health visits, please contact me immediately.

Again, congratulations, and we wish you a long, healthy life.

Sincerely,

(Dr. your name)

Appendix 2
Strategic Plan Example B

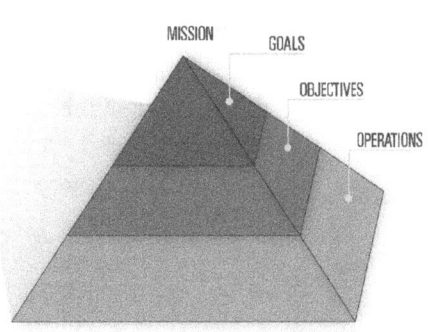

This plan is an example of the structure of the strategic plan for a multidisciplinary clinic with a traditional chiropractic family practice as well as complementary services and a research agenda. Many of the components are similar or identical to those in Appendix 1; however, the differences and additions may give you some ideas for your own plan. Note the naming and numbering system as described in the text. Objectives without an operational task (for example, A4) in fact become the operational task. This strategic plan is larger than average, with 9 goals, 28 objectives, and 150 operational tasks.

Vision
Our vision is universal access to high-quality chiropractic care

Mission
Our mission and purpose is to adjust, educate, and assist as many people as possible toward optimum health and wellness through chiropractic and natural health care. Our practice is characterized by the delivery of highly skilled chiropractic adjustments within a truly caring atmosphere, as well as education and research about chiropractic and the healing process.

Goals

Administrative Division

A. *Office management and physical plant*
   To successfully manage our office and physical plant to support our mission (Statistic: total office visits per month)

B. *Accounting*

To control costs and maximize revenue to provide resources for the survival and growth of the practice and staff
(Statistic: fees charged and collected per month)

C. *Human resources*

To successfully manage our human resources to support our mission
(Statistic: staff turnover rate per year; goal: 0 percent)

D. *Professional sales and supplies*

To sell products and supplies that complement our chiropractic practice
(Statistic: net sales profits per month)

Health-Care Delivery Division

E. *Chiropractic services*

To deliver the highest quality of chiropractic care to all patients
(Statistic: office visit average; goal: 40 or more)

F. *Complementary services*

To deliver complementary natural healing methods, practices, and programs that complement and support our mission
(Statistic: nonchiropractic services delivered per month)

Research and Education Division

G. *Patient Education*

To develop patient education programs as well as a passionate, charismatic atmosphere that will attract new patient referrals from our existing patients
(Statistic: referred NPs per month)

H. *Public education*

To effectively promote the chiropractic story to the entire world, the result of which will be a constant supply of new patients
(Statistic: non-referred NPs per month)

I. *Research program*

To develop an ongoing research agenda that supports the chiropractic profession as well as our mission
(Statistic: number of professional papers published per year)

Objectives and Operational Tasks

A1 To use effective communication techniques in all office communications

    A1a Use effective telephone techniques, including appropriate scripts.

    A1b Use effective standards for appearance and presentation of office, doctors, and staff.

    A1c Develop a unique style and logo for use on all stationary, forms, uniforms, and other practice materials.

    A1d Develop a complete set of up-to-date, first-class forms for patient and office use.

    A1e Develop appropriate scripts for staff and doctor to use in specific circumstances.

A2 To utilize effective and efficient appointment scheduling procedures

    A2a Refine and develop effective new patient procedures, including an educational and informational package for new patients.

    A2b Use multiple appointment program (MAP) whenever possible.

    A2c Instill in patients the need to keep their appointments and follow through with recommended care.

    A2d Call all missed appointments within 15 minutes to reschedule, and keep log of all missed appointments and results of efforts to reschedule.

    A2e Have an appropriate computer system for keeping appointments and financial records.

A3 To have an effective physical plant to support our mission

    A3a Ensure that office is visible via appropriate signs.

        A3b1 Ensure a noteworthy and educational reception room through decoration and accessories.

            A3b1a Create an attractive and safe children's area.

        A3b2 Ensure a fully functional and clean reception desk and work area.

    A3c Establish a properly furnished and equipped patient education center for reports of finding.

- A3d Determine clinical needs and furnish examination and treatment rooms with appropriate equipment and supplies.
- A3e Establish specific room functions and names (for example, examination room, adjustment room, and patient education center) and use the office tour as part of every NP's orientation.
- A3f Establish a routine method of physical plant review, and identify the actual needs of the physical plant as well as a maintenance schedule and standards (that is, use a monthly checklist).
- A3g Establish regular office hours and ensure that these are clearly visible.

A4 To define all office policies in a current manual, including financial policy, appointment policy, employment policy, roles for specific CAs, staff meetings, and other policies as required

B1 To maintain an efficient and effective fee schedule and collection system designed to minimize accounts receivable
- B1a Establish a fee schedule for all services rendered and a catalog of services and products sold.
- B1b Establish, as part of an overall fee schedule, special fees for unique groups.
   - B1b1 Company chiropractor program
   - B1b2 Charity cases; establish criteria and fixed fees
   - B1b3 Family fees
- B1c Establish firm front-desk procedure and control methods, including financial consultation by CA at report of findings.
- B1d Establish firm policy for overdue accounts.

B2 To develop specialized fee arrangements and tracking systems for workers' compensation and personal injury patients
- B2a Establish method of tracking workers' compensation accounts and ensure appropriate billing procedures.
- B2b Establish method of tracking personal injury accounts and ensure appropriate and timely billing procedures.

B2c Establish an insurance file containing names of friendly companies and agents—those that approve direct billing, for example.

B3 Keep fee schedule current and review fees to effectively charge for all services rendered

B3a Perform annual fee review of local competitors.

B3b Establish annual review of all fees, services, and policies.

B3c Establish annual review of office expenses to maximize effectiveness and minimize overhead.

B4 To engage the services of a competent accountant to perform an annual financial review and statement of income and expenses

B4a In consultation with the accountant, determine the most appropriate method of accounting for office receivables and payables.

Professional staff

C1 To define all professional standards and policies in an operational manual for professional staff, including standards of practice, patient protocols, and communications standards such as scripts and standards for professional development.

C2 To perform an annual review of all professional staff and to ensure that they are supportive of and contributing to the mission of the practice

C2a Create professional associate policy requiring associates to attend at least one continuing education or motivational seminar annually.

C2b Determine appropriate format for interviewing and reviewing professional associates on an annual basis.

C3 To develop (or locate elsewhere) appropriate postgraduate and professional programs that provide ongoing professional and personal development

C3a Enroll in appropriate postgraduate and continuing education courses on a regular basis.

C3b Develop a continuing education course to teach through an accredited chiropractic college.

Nonprofessional staff

C4 To engage the services of necessary and relevant staff members

    C4a Conduct a needs assessment of office procedures to determine exactly what staff positions are required.

    C4b Advertise locally and determine hiring criteria and salary levels to be offered.

    C4c Ensure that successful candidates for positions in the office are cognizant of and supportive of the mission of the practice.

C5 To perform an annual review of all staff and ensure that they are supportive of and contributing to the mission of the practice

    C5a Create employment policy requiring staff to attend at least one continuing education or motivational seminar annually.

    C5b Determine appropriate format for interviewing and reviewing staff on an annual basis.

C6 To ensure that all staff operate in a congenial and collegial manner, always fostering a spirit of cooperation and passion for chiropractic

    C6a Have at least two off-premises staff get togethers each year.

    C6b Resolve staff conflicts quickly and create open atmosphere for communication.

    C6c Hold weekly meetings and training sessions for all staff.

D1 To determine, using questionnaires, interviews, and feedback forms, what health products are in demand by our patients

    D1a Devise and use patient-feedback questionnaires.

    D1b Interview selected patients for information about product sales in our office.

D2 To determine what health products are necessary for our patients as complements to our practice

    D2a Meet with professional staff to determine list of products to offer in practice.

D3 To locate wholesale sources of the products we intend to market and sell

D4 To set up an attractive health product section in our office, complete with amechanism for ordering, stocking, displaying, selling, and tracking the sales of these products

    D4a Determine location for health products section.

    D4b Obtain necessary accounting system for maintaining sales and inventory records.

    D4c Assign staff member to be in charge of stocking, ordering, and tracking supplies.

    D4d Decide on advertising policy and methods to market products.

E1 To develop and offer high-quality patient care programs (to remove quality interference to practice growth)

    E1a Develop new patient programs.

        E1a1 Develop a formal new patient information kit to be given to all new patients.

        E1a2 Develop and use a thorough and personalized consultation and examination format for all new patients.

            E1a2a Ensure that examination room is fully equipped with necessary and up-to-date equipment and supplies.

            E1a2b Arrange for radiology facilities or create radiology department in the clinic.

        E1a3 Develop a report of findings package that includes a doctor's manual of sequenced diagrams in a binder and a written report for patients covering the total health package (pain relief, restoral of health, maintenance/elective care); also include a letter sent to all new patients after their report of findings.

        (An example of a letter to be sent to new patients after their report of findings is shown on page 132–133.)

            E1a3a Develop a formal report after reassessments similar to the one used for E1a3.

            E1a3b Develop a formal initial patient education program (several objectives over the first four visits: subluxation, adjustment, families, health restoration, and lifetime maintenance).

E1a3c Develop a method for contacting, educating, and reactivating patients who do not return for care after their report of findings.

E1a4 Always promptly acknowledge and thank referral sources.

E1b Develop regular patient programs.

E1b1 Be familiar with as many treatment systems as possible and specialize in various aspects of some of these.

E1b2 Be knowledgeable of all major exercise programs related to major pain syndromes.

E1b3 Regularly keep up with all paperwork such as insurance reports and referral letters.

E1b4 Keep patients enthusiastic about their care, throughout their care program, by using an ongoing tableside educational system.

E1b5 Develop and use regular reexamination protocols and systems that provide for objective measurement of improvement.

E1b5a Develop and use specific protocols and forms for reexamination of patients in specific categories, such as whiplash, pregnancy, headache, low back pain, and others.

E1b6 Define and develop areas of specialty interest (for example, sports care, pediatrics, pregnancy, and geriatrics).

E1b7 Be familiar with modern chiropractic and natural methods of acute and chronic pain control.

E1b8 Be familiar with basic nutritional supplementation as related to the needs of chiropractic patients.

E1b9 Establish appropriate referral networks with local professionals.

E2 To develop and use an effective system of health review, promotion, and maintenance (remove quantity interference to practice growth)

E2a Develop maintenance/elective care programs.

E2a1 Develop a special procedure for initiation of maintenance care (for example, special letter congratulating patient, specialized health promotion material, VIP mailings, and discounts on purchases of supplies). (An example of a letter to a patient who is beginning maintenance care is shown on page 117.)

E2a2 Develop an ongoing educational system to keep patients motivated to continue in a maintenance program.

E2b   Develop family health promotion and review.

    E2b1   Develop and use forms and protocols for regular collection of family health data.

        E2b1a   Family registration form for all new patients

        E2b1b   Semiannual family health questionnaire (stresses need for doctor to know all family health problems)

    E2b2   Use mechanism and procedure for screening all children of patients for scoliosis, postural distortion, and subluxations.

E2c   Develop reactivation and recall procedures.

    E2c1   Develop and use a routine method of recall and reactivation of inactive patients.

        E2c1a   Recall (short term): Develop specific method and phone scripts to use with patients who have missed a scheduled appointment.

        E2c1b   Reactivation (long term): Develop a method, including a letter and phone script, to be used on a regular basis to contact inactive patients. (See pages 91–95 for some information and research findings on patient reactivation.)

F1   To determine and provide the natural health services and practices necessary to complement our practice

    F1a   Determine the standards of practice required of natural health practitioners in our clinic.

    F1b   Advertise to hire the appropriate practitioners (suggested providers include massage therapists, naturopathic doctors, homeopathic doctors, and acupuncturists).

    F1c   Create, with attorney, a suitable contract form for professional associates.

    F1d   Determine the best method of remuneration (percentage or salary).

    F1e   Develop a training program to ensure that all complementary providers understand and support the mission of the practice.

    F1f   Develop training programs and grand rounds to encourage professional teamwork and collegial behavior.

    F1g   Determine methods for tracking performance and requirements of complementary health providers.

G1 To develop an effective long-range internal marketing and education program

- G1a Hold a quarterly staff conference, off premises, to review and formulate patient education programs and internal marketing action plans.
- G1b Use internal marketing research methods to determine what our patients want and demand (including patient feedback questionnaires and patient focus groups).
- G1c Develop a formal training program for our office staff, both professional and nonprofessional, on the methods of educating our patients and marketing our services internally.

G2 To develop and implement specific patient education programs that will motivate our patients and attract new patient referrals from our existing patients

- G2a Develop a referral management program.
  - G2a1 Ask for referrals. Develop scripts and practice them. Develop patient recruiting package and special procedures and offers for family members.
  - G2a2 Have up-to-date brochure-style curriculum vitae in reception room, as well as other materials that encourage referral behavior.
  - G2a3 Have practice brochure and NP kit.
  - G2a4 Engage in internal prospecting activities on a daily basis, such as encouraging patients to discuss the health needs of their families and friends.
  - G2a5 Create a frequent referrer program.
    - G2a5a Telephone acknowledgment
    - G2a5b Note and gift
    - G2a5c Send all gifts with a powerful letter
  - G2a6 Develop specific methods for recording all referral sources and immediately and effectively acknowledging referrals.
  - G2a7 Ask suitable patients for written testimonials, and collect these in a booklet available in the reception room.
- G2b Develop a patient education program.
  - G2b1 Obtain or develop and use patient information sheets on a variety of topics especially related to our clinic and our clinical approach to health conditions that also motivate our patients toward a wellness lifestyle.

- G2b2 Develop regular informational mailings to patients and referral sources.
  - G2b2a Regular quarterly newsletter
  - G2b2b VIP mailing (occasional)
  - G2b2c Other informational bulletins
  - G2b2d Information bulletins and reprints to referring physicians
- G2b3 Ensure that educational material is available throughout the office.
- G2b4 Determine schedule and system for providing regular tableside educational material and information.
- G2b5 Create a patient lending library of relevant books and videos.
- G2b6 Create and maintain a bulletin board of relevant articles in the reception room.

G2c Develop a spinal care class.
- G2c1 Develop and use a weekly meeting on chiropractic and the healing process.
- G2c2 Develop and use a specific procedure for informing patients of the spinal care class and obtaining a commitment to attend the class.

G2d Offer other internal promotions.
- G2d1 Use unusual promotion dates to generate enthusiasm.
  - G2d1a Ethnic holidays
  - G2d1b Office anniversaries (try to have something each month)
  - G2d1c Seasonal and thematic dates (for example, Christmas and Halloween)
  - G2d1d Monthly "children's day" on a weekend
- G2d2 Have an annual patient appreciation event in the office.

H1 **To develop an effective long-range external marketing program**
- H1a Use a community advisory panel of local people to meet with us on a quarterly basis and discuss our role in the community.
- H1b Use external marketing research methods to determine what our public wants and demands.
- H1c Develop a formal public relations program, including press contacts and methodology for press releases.

H2 To develop an annual marketing calendar

    H2a Develop a specific annual marketing calendar, incorporating all prioritized activities relating to marketing and patient education.

H3 To develop routine procedural promotions that educate our community about chiropractic and natural healing

    H3a Promote our services through joint efforts with others.

        H3a1 Develop joint promotion and networking efforts with local non-competing professionals.

    H3b Promote our services through written media.

        H3b1 Write articles for local papers on newsworthy topics.

        H3b2 Seek opportunity to write column each week for one or more newspapers.

        H3b3 Develop a local newspaper advertising program.

        H3b4 Develop a yellow pages advertising program.

        H3b4 Create and distribute a neighborhood flyer on a quarterly basis.

        H3b5 Promote our practice by distributing at least five business cards daily.

    H3c Promote our services through regular miscellaneous promotions.

        H3c1 Develop corporate wellness program and market it to local industry.

        H3c2 Develop school posture program with local PTA.

        H3c3 Hold seasonal fund-raising promotions to support local charities.

        H3c4 Identify local fund-raising opportunities to assist and support (such as fun runs).

H4 To develop special promotions that educate our community about chiropractic and natural healing

    H4a Promote our services through speaking engagements and public appearances.

	H4a1	Promote and deliver public lectures on various topics related to chiropractic and the healing process.
	H4a2	Develop a public-speaking agenda (major topics only) with targeted audiences. (Plan six speeches per year for 3 years.)
	H4a3	Develop spinal screening programs for use in malls, schools, and health fairs.
	H4a4	Develop a health and wellness speakers' group with other professionals in the community.

H4b Promote our services through special written projects.

    H4b1 Write a small book on chiropractic and wellness.

    H4b2 Consider publishing a small health and wellness newspaper for my community.

H4c Promote our services through special miscellaneous promotions.

    H4c1 Offer $1 million for a hole-in-one at a local charity golf tournament. (Insurance policy can be purchased to cover hole-in-one tournaments.)

    H4c2 Arrange to have an annual open house for the community to visit our clinic.

I1   **To be aware of, support, and contribute to the research and chiropractic literature, including the development of an office research agenda**

    I1a Subscribe to at least one peer-reviewed chiropractic research journal.

    I1b Submit for publication at least one case report per year.

    I1c Submit for publication at least one literature review per year.

    I1d Develop an agenda for a clinic research project.

        I1d1 Contact and consult with local chiropractic college research department.

        I1d2 Determine if our clinic can participate in a larger study involving several clinics.

Here is a copy of the letter sent to new patients after their report of findings.

Dear Patient and Friend:

Thank you for choosing us as your family chiropractors. We look forward to the opportunity to provide the unique benefits of chiropractic health care to you and your family.

As a new chiropractic patient, there are several things we would like you to know. Just as it is important for us to know all about you so we can render a thorough assessment prior to care, so it is important for you to have a good understanding of chiropractic care to get the greatest benefit to your health.

Understanding the Real Value of Chiropractic Care

Some patients, at first, seem to want only pain relief as a benefit of chiropractic care. When it comes right down to it, though, most patients really want a solution to the *cause* of their health problems. Just covering up the symptoms is not the answer—in fact, most chiropractic patients first see their chiropractor because they are fed up with painkillers and heating pads. Chiropractic care seeks the cause of your problem, and the *real* value of chiropractic family care lies in the fact that true health comes from removing the causes of sickness, not in temporarily covering them up. It takes longer to do this, but you're worth it!

Following Our Recommendations

Your health program will be based on experience with similar cases and the expected speed of response of your body to structural correction. You cannot bargain with Mother Nature. Please follow your care program exactly as prescribed. Our experience shows without a doubt that the best results come from a thorough program of care. Don't settle for anything less than this—your health depends on it. Each visit builds on the previous results of structural correction. Missed appointments must be made up because they simply delay your improvement, wasting your time and ours.

Getting Excited About Your Health

With chiropractic care, your body structure will slowly improve. In turn, your body function will improve because your nerves, which control every body function, will no longer be irritated by abnormal body structure, posture, or alignment. Since your body cells continually replace themselves under the control of nerves (in fact, your entire body is renewed every 1 to 2 years), you can say that "you're not getting older, you're getting better" under chiropractic care. This is something to get excited about!

Conditions That Can Be Helped by Chiropractic Care

It is frustrating when people suffer needlessly because they *didn't know* that they might have been helped through chiropractic care. The most important reason to seek chiropractic care is to have your spine examined for the presence of what chiropractors call "subluxations" (spinal misalignments)—and, unfortunately, they do not always cause pain. Therefore, the best reason to see a chiropractor is for a check-up *before symptoms occur*. Everyone in your family should have a chiropractic check-up.

In fact, chiropractic care is wonderfully simple—correcting subluxations (spinal misalignments) using safe and gentle adjustments, by hand, for the purpose of removing interference to the body's ability to heal itself. What happens when you cut your finger? Just watch it heal, literally, before your eyes. This healing power resides within each of us. Chiropractors call it "innate intelligence." Our job is to remove interference to its natural expression in your body. Think about it: Are there really any limits to the healing ability of this inborn intelligence that controls every breath and heartbeat in our body? It is most likely that you had no idea about the "chiropractic story" (as we call it). You probably thought of chiropractic as primarily a treatment of aches and pains. Unfortunately, you are not alone with this limited concept. Listed below are the most common reasons for a new patient to visit a chiropractor:

- Back problems (all types)
- Stress and stress-related conditions
- Whiplash and other forms of neck pain (all car accident victims should see a chiropractor as soon as possible)
- Headaches (tension and migraine)
- Shoulder and arm pains
- Workplace and industrial injuries
- Problems with posture (children, teenagers, and adults)
- Sports injuries (we are also happy to provide advice to teams)
- Nonspecific problems of body function (most commonly seen conditions are asthma, indigestion, allergies, menstrual cramps, and bedwetting)

If in doubt about a specific type of problem, please ask us. *Only* a chiropractor can determine if a particular problem can be helped by chiropractic care.

Your Help Is Needed!

Chiropractic is probably the world's best-kept secret! Perhaps you grew up getting regular chiropractic care, but chances are that you did not know anything about the world's second largest primary care health-care profession until your friend or family member recommended it. Please help us to reach others in need. Within your circle of friends and family are dozens of people suffering needlessly. Please become our "wellness partner" and let's reach out to help whenever we can.

We look forward to seeing you soon and to helping you attain more bountiful health in the future.

Yours sincerely,

Dr. Michael Wiles

Appendix 3

Strategic Plan Template

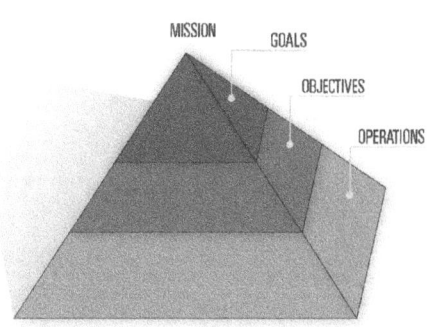

This template may be used as a structural guide as you complete the outline of your strategic plan. Of course, you may have fewer or more goals, objectives, and operational tasks than I have suggested in the template. The template guide reproduced below provides for 5 goals, 20 objectives, and 100 operational tasks. While yours will very likely vary from these numbers, they should give you some idea of the average size of a strategic plan.

Vision

Mission
Our mission and purpose is to...

Appendix 3 Strategic Plan Template

Goals

A

B

C

D

E

Objectives and Operational Tasks

A1

    A1a

    A1b

    A1c

    A1d

    A1e

A2

    A2a

    A2b

    A2c

    A2d

    A2e

A3

    A3a

    A3b

    A3c

    A3d

    A3e

A4

    A4a

    A4b

    A4c

    A4d

    A4e

B1

    B1a

    B1b

    B1c

    B1d

    B1e

B2

    B2a

    B2b

    B2c

    B2d

    B2e

B3

    B3a

    B3b

    B3c

    B3d

    B3e

B4

    B4a

    B4b

    B4c

    B4d

    B4e

C1

    C1a

    C1b

    C1c

    C1d

    C1e

Appendix 3 Strategic Plan Template

C2

    C2a

    C2b

    C2c

    C2d

    C2e

C3

    C3a

    C3b

    C3c

    C3d

    C3e

C4

    C4a

    C4b

    C4c

    C4d

    C4e

D1

    D1a

    D1b

    D1c

    D1d

    D1e

D2

    D2a

    D2b

    D2c

    D2d

    D2e

D3

    D3a

    D3b

    D3c

    D3d

    D3e

D4

    D4a

    D4b

    D4c

    D4d

    D4e

E1

    E1a

    E1b

    E1c

    E1d

    E1e

E2

    E2a

    E2b

    E2c

    E2d

    E2e

E3

    E3a

    E3b

    E3c

    E3d

    E3e

E4

    E4a

    E4b

    E4c

    E4d

    E4e

Appendix 4

Executive Summary of Steps to Create Your Strategic Plan

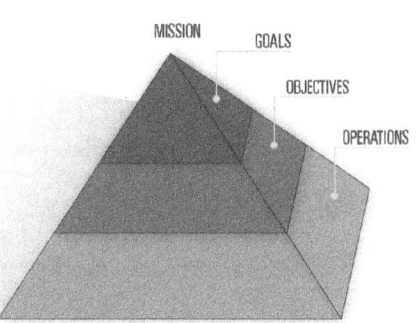

1. Create a vision statement.
2. Create a mission statement.
3. Create strategic goals from your mission statement.
4. For each strategic goal, create tactical objectives.
5. For each tactical objective, create operational plans.
6. Divide operational plans into standing plans and single-use plans.
7. Divide single-use plans into programs and projects.
8. Divide standing plans into rules, procedures, and policies.
9. Prioritize the operational plans using either tactical prioritization (see step 10) or operational prioritization (see step 12).
10. For tactical prioritization, determine your overall time frame and divide up your prioritized tactical objectives into smaller time segments. (Suggested overall time frame is 6 months to 5 years, and suggested smaller time segments are 1 month to 1 year. If in doubt, try a 5-year plan with 1-year subsegments.) Go to step 11.
11. Take your list of tactical priorities for the first subsegment of time and further subdivide this list into 1-month periods of time. For each tactical objective in these 1-month periods, list and prioritize all their operational tasks. (Keep a separate prioritized list of single-use plans, and organize your standing plans into rules and regulations, procedures, and policies.) Go to step 16.

12. For operational prioritization, create a list of all single-use plans. Go to step 13.

13. Create a list of all standing plans and subdivide them, as you are able, into rules and regulations, procedures and policies. Go to step 14.

14. Prioritize your single-use plans and determine your overall time frame for completion of these plans. Then subdivide this list into smaller time segments. (Suggested overall time frame is 6 months to 5 years, and suggested smaller time segments are 1 month to 1 year. If in doubt, try a 5-year plan with 1-year subsegments.) Go to step 15.

15. Place all your standing plans in a binder entitled Manual of Standard Operating Procedures. Go to step 16.

16. From your standing plans only, make a list of all daily, weekly, monthly, or yearly action steps. To this list add daily or weekly tasks of a personal nature that affect your professional practice. Be sure to include, as one of your weekly tasks, "scheduled programs and projects" (that is, your prioritized single-use plans). From these lists, construct a Daily Critical Action Checklist.

17. Review your entire plan for omissions and for feasibility (in other words, do a reality check). If necessary, take the time to rewrite sections for consistency, relevance, and congruence with the overall vision and mission.

18. Get to work! Review your plan daily and take the important step of finding quiet time each day to visualize your overall plan unfolding as it should. In other words, what began with a vision is fueled daily by visualization. Have passion for your plan. If you begin to feel you are losing this passion, it is time to review the plan in its entirety. This is your plan—based on your own vision—and it should give you a feeling of incredible power, passion, and excitement. At the very least, take a few days each year to quietly review the entire planning process. I suggest a retreat to your favorite location for relaxation and spiritual rejuvenation.

I would end by wishing you good luck, but frankly, luck has nothing to do with it. Your plan, followed passionately and with discipline and consistency, is the best guarantee of success you will ever need or ever have.

Index

A

Ability, 99
Above-down planning, 101
Accountability, importance of, 81
Accounts, in strategic plan example, 106
Acknowledging patients, 90
Action
  mission-oriented, xii
  success and, 2
  translating dream into reality through, 50
Action course, congruency and choice of, 54
Action steps, 51
  using numbering and lettering scheme for, 54
Adaptability
  for practice, 1–2
  stability *vs.*, 9–10
Adaptation, 34
Administrative division, goals within, 45
Affability, 99, 100
American Medical Association, 99
American Medical News, 99
Amiel, Henri Frederic, 59
Annual marketing calendar, 96
  in strategic plan example, 112
Annual program of care, 36
Apathy, 33
Appointments
  reactivation program and, 92–95
  scheduling of, in strategic plan example, 107
Assertiveness, 100
Assets, 8
Attitude, 8
Availability, 99

B

Balance, objectives and, 32
Baruch, Bernard, 81
Big picture, understanding, 7
Block, Peter, 13
Board of directors, industrial planning and, 4
Brainstorming
  description of, 28
  operational level planning and, 54
Buddha, 49
Budgets, 52. *See also* Fees as kind of single-use plan, 50

C

CA. *See* Chiropractic assistant
Canadian Memorial Chiropractic College (Toronto), mission statement of, 21–22
Cantor, Eddie, 63
Carlyle, Thomas, xii
Cash flow, 8
Challenges, in planning, 12
Cheerfulness, 100
Chesterfield, Lord, 101
Chiropractic, visual representation of your passion for, 15
Chiropractic assistants, 3
  reactivation program, results of 570 follow-up calls by, 93*t*
Chiropractic education, planning and, 4
Chiropractic practices, mission statement examples from, 20–21
Chiropractic students, mission statement examples from, 20–21

---

page numbers followed by "t" or "f" denote tables or figures respectively

Chiropractors
  fee-related issues and mistakes made by, 97–99
  visioning by, 14
Clinical results, 8
Collaboration, 34
Communication techniques, in strategic plan example, 106–107
Compassion, 100
Competitive advantage, 7
Competitors, 9–10
Complex strategic plans, management of, 44–48
Congruence, reviewing grand strategic plan for, 69
Continuing education, 83
Controls, statistics and, 11
Coordinative planning, 31
Cover page, for manual of standard operating procedures, 79
Critical action list, 50
Critical daily action steps, 55
Critical lists, prioritized list of, 77
Cybernetic management system, 50
Cybernetic systems, organizations as, 11

D

Daily action checklist, 79
Daily critical action checklist, 52
  example of, 85t
Daily critical action steps, 81–85
  creating list for, 81
Daily preparation, 83
Darwin, Charles, 68
Dating, of planning documents, 72
DC (discipline plus consistency), 78, 81
Decision making, 64
Decisions
  successful practices and, 19
  types of, 65t
Democratic method, 65
Desire, successful practices and, 19
Direction, successful practices and, 19
Divisional goals, 44
Divisions, 48
  large set of goals grouped into, 44–48
  three, planning pyramid with, as described in text, 47
Doctor, as chief cook and bottle washer, 10–11
Doing, action steps, 52

Dreams, translation of, into reality, 50–52
Drucker, Peter, 34
Dynamic plan, 9–10

E

Economic factors, mission statement and, 18
Economy of action, 50
Education, marketing and, 48
Educational planning, 4
  levels of, 4t
Efficiency, 28
Eisenhower, Dwight, 23
Electronic file folders, 55
Emergencies, fees and, 99
Empathy, 100
Employee satisfaction, 28
Environmental constraints, 33
Established practices
  prioritization approach to take with, 63–64
  tactical prioritization—execution plan A for, 64–72
Ethical constraints, 33
Execution, of action steps, 52
Executive folder, 55
Exercise, 83
Expression of intent, 17
External constraints, 33
External factors, in long-range planning, 8–9
External marketing program, in strategic plan example, 106

F

Family health promotion and review, in strategic plan example, 111
Fee arrangements, in strategic plan example, 108–109
Fees, 88, 96, 97–99
  apologizing for, 97
  being vague or evasive about, 98
  discussing with the wrong person, 98
  in strategic plan example, 106
Fee schedule
  keeping current, 109
  in strategic plan example, 108
File folders, numbered or electronic, 55
Filing cabinet, executive folder in, 55
Final preparations, 87–101
Finances, 8

First-level management, 49
First-period objectives, distributing operational tasks associated with, into smaller time periods, 71
First things first, doing, 63–79
Fiscal constraints, 33
Free lectures, 116
Frequent referrer program, 113
Future scenarios, alternative, 9

G

Goals, 1, 2, 31, 63
  creating first objectives for fulfillment of, 34
  defined, 25
  first, dissection of into component objectives, 36–37
  larger-than-usual set of, grouped into divisions, 44–48
  statements for, 30
  strategic, 28
  in strategic plan, 105
  in strategic plan example, 105–106
  ten, planning pyramid with, as described in text, 47
  ten, within planning pyramid from example in text, 47
  vision statement and, 17
Goethe, Johann Wolfgang von, 104
Grading scale, prioritizing tactical objectives and, 65–67
Grand strategic plan, continual reviewing of, 69
Grinde, Bob, 98
Group decision making, 64

H

Health-care delivery division, goals within, 45
Health review system, in strategic plan example, 111
Helvetius, Claude Adrien, 16
Hill, Napoleon, ix
Holmes, Oliver Wendell, Jr., 61
Honesty, planning process and, 8
Howard, Vernon, 89
Hubbard, Elbert, 87
Hugo, Victor, 84
Huxley, Thomas, 62

I

I care attitude (ICA), 110
Identification, of organization, 33
Inactive patients, phone calls made to, 92
Indexes
  for manual of standard operating procedures, 79
  for planning documents, 72
Industrial planning, 4–5
  levels of, $4t$
Industry, 100
Inefficiency, 50
Information, movement of, in large organizations, 49–50
Information retrieval, 55
Inspirational reading, 83
Institutional mission statements, examples of, 21–23
Insurance file, establishing, 109
Integration, 33
Integrative objectives, 32
Internal constraints, 33
Internal factors, in long-range planning, 8
Internal marketing program, in strategic plan example, 106, 112
Internal promotions, in strategic plan example, 115

J

Janse, Joseph, 13
Joint promotion efforts, in strategic plan example, 116
Journaling, ix

K

Kids Klinics, 112
Kindness, 100
Knowledge, 8

L

Lao Tzu, 31, 103
Lavater, Johann Kaspar, 57
Lectures, free, 116
Legal constraints, 33
Legal environment, 8
Lettering system
  action steps and use of, 54
  in text, explanation of, 48

Index

Liabilities, 8
Lincoln, Abraham, 12
Lists
  of critical daily action steps, 81
  of programs and projects, 78
Literature, promoting our services through, 115
Long-range planning, description of, 7–8
Long-range planning issues, 7–12
  adaptability *vs.* stability: dynamic plan, 9–10
  challenges related to, 12
  controls and statistics and, 11
  for doctor, 10–11
  external factors, 8–9
  internal factors, 8
  time and reality, 9

M

Mail media, promoting our services through, 115
Maimonedes, 97
Maintenance/elective care programs, in strategic plan example, 111
Maintenance letter, copy of, 117
Managed care, 9
Management by objectives, 33, 34
Manual of standard operating procedures, creating, 79
Manuals of operation, 52
MAP. *See* Multiple appointment program
Marketing
  education and, 48
  in strategic plan example, 106
Marketing budget, in strategic plan example, 112
Marketing calendar, annual, 96, 112
Material resources, 8
McGannon, Donald, 58
Measurement, of objectives, 35
Mental preparation, 83
Mertz, C. J., 95
Middle management, 49, 50
Middle-management level, tactical and operational planning at, 10
Military planning, 3
  levels of, 3*t*
Mission, 13–23, 63
  rewriting statement for, 26
  strategic planning pyramid and, 2

Mission statements, 2, 32.
  See also Vision statements
  careful drafting of, 10
  complex strategic plan example, 45
  creating, 16–23
  examples of, from chiropractic practices and chiropractic students, 20–21
  exercises related to analysis of, 28–30
  from, to strategic goals, 27–28
  future and, 26
  industrial planning and, 4
  regular review of, 9
  in strategic plan example, 105
Monthly critical action list, 52
Monthly schedule of promotional events, 96
Multiple appointment program, 107
Multiple referrals, rewarding, 113

N

Name tags, 51
Neighborhood flyers, 115
New patient consultation and examination, fees and, 98–99
New patient procedures, 88, 89
New practices
  organizational prioritization—execution plan B for, 72–79
  prioritization approach to take with, 63, 64
Newsletters, 96
Northwestern Health Science University, mission statement of, 22–23
NP kits, 113
  developing, 107, 109
Numbered file folders, 55
Numbering, of planning documents, 72
Numbering system
  action steps and use of, 54
  for operational plans, 56
  in text, explanation of, 48

O

Objectives, 1, 2, 11, 25, 31
  characteristics of, 32–34
  first, creation of, 33, 34–42
  identification of, 54
  identifying key elements of, 54
  listing action steps based on, 55
  measurement of, writing statistics for, 38–42

Index

scoring of, for importance, 67*t*
in strategic plan, 105
in strategic plan example, 106–116
thirty four, within planning pyramid from example in text, 47
Office communication techniques, new patient procedures and, 89
Office management goals, in strategic plan example, 105
Office policies, in strategic plan example, 108
Office procedures, 8
Office visit average, 35
Operating management, 49
Operating supervisors, 49
Operational activities, 5
Operational planning, xi, 5, 19
levels of, 3, 31, 49–62
middle-management level and, 10
Operational plans, 63
creating, 53–55
developing set of, 57–62
five-step process in formulation of, 54–55
listing of, with given structural format and numbering system, 56
Operational tasks
creating list of single-use plans from list of, 74–75
creating list of standing plans from list of, and categorizing as rules, regulations, procedures and policies, 76
prioritization based on, 63
in strategic plan, 105
in strategic plan example, 106–116
Operations
one hundred and two, planning pyramid with, as described in text, 47
one hundred and two, within planning pyramid from example in text, 47
Opportunities, recognizing, 7
Optimal health, 34
Organizational prioritization, execution plan B—recommended for new practices, 72–79
Organizations, five primary objectives of, 33–34
Organizing plans, 55–62
Osler, Sir William, 52
Outcome measures, 8

P

Palmer, B. J., 72
Parker, James, 111
Parker, Karl, 19
Passion, 101
Patient appreciation days, 113
Patient care programs, in strategic plan example, 109–110
Patient education programs, developing, 114
Patient referrals, 8
Patients
inactive, phone calls made to, 92
reasons given for not keeping appointments by, 94–95
regular visit procedures and, 90–91
Patient satisfaction, 8
Patient visit average, 35
Performance, of action steps, 52
Persistence, professional success and, 101
Personal injury patients, fee arrangements and tracking systems of, 108–109
Personality, professional success and, 100
Personal strategic goals, 21
Personnel constraints, 33
Peters, Lawrence J., 60
Peters, Thomas, 16
Philosophy, professional success and, 100–101
Physical plant, 8
goals for, in strategic plan example, 105
in strategic plan example, 107–108
Physical preparation, 83
Pioneer planning levels, 5*t*
Pioneers in new land, survival of, 5
Planning
challenges in, 12
educational, 4
industrial, 4–5
military, 3
operational level of, 3, 19, 31, 49–62
professional success and, 101
strategical, 19
strategical level of, 31
tactical, 19
tactical level of, 2–3
Planning documents
development of, for practice, 1–2
example of, for two, 2-month periods, 73*t*

for subdivided time periods, 72
Planning pyramid
  from example in text, 47
  mission at top of, 13
  with three divisions, as described in text, 47
Planning study, plan vs., 12
Plan(s), 1
  defined, 1
  organizing, 55–62
Policy(ies), 1, 5, 51, 52, 53, 55, 63, 72
  final preparations and, 87
  list of critical daily action steps and, 81
  list of standing plans and categorization of items as, 76
  within manual of standard operating procedures, 79
  separating standing plans into, 74
Political environment, 8
Political factors, mission statement and, 18
Practice mission, statement of, 19
Prepractice briefing, 83, 84
Present time consciousness, 110
Preventive maintenance care, 36
Prioritization
  of single-use plans, from most important to least important, 78
  of standing plans, 79
Priority planning document, 70
Procedure manuals, 51
Procedure(s), 1, 5, 51, 52, 53, 55, 63, 72
  final preparations and, 87
  list of critical daily action steps and, 81
  list of standing plans and categorization of items as, 76
  new patient, 88, 89
  professional success and, 101
  promotions and, 95
  recall and reactivation, 88, 91–95
  regular visit, 88, 89–91
  separating standing plans into, 74
  types of, in strategic plan, 88
Procrastination, 33
Production, 28
Products and services, contracts for, and course of action, xii
Professional designations, 51
Professional history, realistic appraisal of, 9
Professional success, five Ps of, 99–101
Programs, 52
  list of, 78
  in single-use plans, 50, 77
Progress examinations, 36

Progress notes, 90
Project HOPE (Health Opportunity by Periodic Evaluation), 111
Project(s), 52
  list of, 78
  in single-use plans, 50, 77
Promotional activities, 88
Promotional events, planning, 96
Promotion of services, in strategic plan example, 115–116
Promotions, 95–97
  categorizing, 96, 97
PTC. *See* Present time consciousness
Public appearances, promoting services through, 116
Purpose statement, 13
  developing, 16
PVA. See Patient visit average

Q

Quality care delivery, in strategic plan example, 106
Quarterly objectives, 5
Quarterly schedule of promotional events, 96

R

Reactivation, 51, 91
Reactivation and recall procedures, in strategic plan example, 111
Reactivation letter, 92
Reactivation program, results of 570 follow-up phone calls by four chiropractic assistants and, 93t
Recall, 51
Recall and reactivation procedures, 88, 91–95
Reed, Scott, 53
Referral management program, developing, 113–114
Regular business hours, 100
Regular patient programs, developing, 110
Regular visit procedures, 88, 89–91
  suggested format for, 90–91
Regulations, 51, 63, 72
  list of standing plans and categorization of items as, 76
  within manual of standard operating procedures, 79
Relevance, reviewing grand strategic plan for, 69
Report of findings, 109

Research and education division, goals within, 46
Reviewing daily plan, 83
Revitalization, 34
Robbins, Anthony, 52
ROF. *See* Report of findings
Roosevelt, Franklin, 23
Roosevelt, Theodore, 95
Rule(s), 5, 50, 52, 55, 63, 72
   defined, 51
   list of critical daily action steps and, 81
   list of standing plans and categorization of items as, 76
   within manual of standard operating procedures, 79
   separating standing plans into, 74

S

Salespeople, contacting, xii
Scenarios, developing, 54
Scheduled programs and projects, as daily action steps, 83
Scoring, of objectives, for importance, 67t
Seneca, 7
Shared decision making, 64, 65
Shaw, George Bernard, 5
Single-use plans, 50, 52, 53, 63, 77, 83
   creating list of, from list of operational tasks, 74–75
   identifying items on operational list as either standing plan or, 74
   prioritization of, from most important to least important, 78
Skills, 8
Social factors, mission statement and, 18
Soviet Union (former), 5-year planning in, 5
Speaking engagements, 96
   promoting services through, 116
Specialized programs, 96
   promoting services through, 116
Spinal care classes, developing, 114–115
Stability, 25
   adaptability *vs.*, 9–10
Staff meetings, weekly, 83
Stakeholders, mission statement and, 18
Standard operating procedures, 51
Standing plans, 50, 52, 53, 63
   identifying items on operational list as either single-use plan or, 74
   making list of daily and weekly action steps from, 81–82

prioritizing, 79
Statistics, 35
   controls and, 11
   measurement of objectives and writing of, 38–42
   using, 43–44
Stone, W. Clement, 103–104
Strategic goals, 28, 63
   from mission statement to, 27–28
   as source of measurable statistic, 43
   statement of, 30
   writing tactical objectives for, 38–42
Strategic planning, xi, 1–5, 19
   level of, 25–30, 31
Strategic planning pyramid, 2, 9
Strategic plans
   complex, management of, 44–48
   determining time limits for, 68–69
   example of, 105–116
   suggested minimum components of, 88–89
   time span for, 9
Strategic plan template, 56
Strategies, 1
Strategy formulation, 49
Strategy implementation, 49
Strengths
   capitalizing on, 7
   identifying, 8
Strengths, weaknesses, opportunities, and threats. *See* SWOT analysis
Stress, decision-making process and, 65
Subdivided time periods, planning documents for, 72
Success, components of, 2
Survival, 28
SWOT analysis, 7–8, 9
Systems theory, 11

T

Tactical objectives, 63
   grading scale and prioritizing of, 65–67
   prioritization based on, 63
   writing for strategic goals, 38–42
Tactical planning, xi, 19
   description of, 31
   level of, 2–3, 31–48
   middle-management level and, 10
   time period for, 5
Tactical prioritization, execution plan A—for existing and established practices, 64–72

Tactics, 1
Team members, average ranking scores of 14 objectives by, 68*t*
Teamwork
  decision matrix and, 64–65, 65*t*
  tactical prioritization and, 64
Technical constraints, 33
Technological factors, mission statement and, 18
Telephone technique, new patient procedures and, 89
Thoreau, Henry David, 18
Threats, knowledge of, 7
Time limits, determining for strategic plan, 68–69
Time span, for strategic plan, 9
Torah, ix
Training sessions, 83
Two, 2-month periods, example of planning document for, 73*t*
Type I decisions, 64, 65*t*
Type II decisions, 64, 65*t*
Type III decisions, 64, 65*t*
Type IV decisions, 65, 65*t*

U

Understanding, 100
Urgencies, fees and, 99

V

Val-Pack, 116
VIP mailings, 111
Vision, 13–23, 63
  definitions of, 14
  journeying toward, 103
  operational plan and, 53
  proper strategic planning and, xi
  rewriting statement for, 26
  strategic planning pyramid and, 2
Vision statements, 32, 103.
  See also Mission statements
  careful drafting of, 10
  complex strategic plan example, 45
  creating, 13–16
  distant future and, 26
  example of development of, 17
  examples of, 14
  exercises
    related to creation of, 15, 16
    related to development of, 17, 18–19
  in strategic plan example, 105
Visit procedures, regular, 88
Visualization, 103–104

W

Waste, 50
Weaknesses, identifying, 7, 8
Weekly schedule of promotional events, 96
Weekly staff meetings, 83
West, Mae, 99
Wiles, Michael, 48, 78
Workers' compensation, fee arrangements and tracking systems of, 108–109
World War II, 3, 10, 17, 23
Worthy goals, success and, 2
Writing, art of, ix
Written media, promoting services through, 115

Y

Yearly critical action list, 52
Yearly schedule of promotional events, 96

www.ingramcontent.com/pod-product-compliance
Lightning Source LLC
LaVergne TN
LVHW011708060526
838200LV00051B/2814